CW00829462

A NOBLE TASK

Eldership and Ministry in the local Church

NEIL SUMMERTON

THE PATERNOSTER PRESS
Carlisle UK

Copyright © Neil Summerton 1987, 1990
Second Edition 1994

*All Rights Reserved. No part of this publication may
be reproduced, stored in a retrieval system, or
transmitted, in any form or by any means, electronic,
mechanical, photocopying, recording or otherwise,
without the prior permission of the publisher
or a licence permitting restricted copying.
In the U.K. such licences are issued by the
Copyright Licensing Agency, 90 Tottenham Court Road,
London W1P 9HE.*

*This book is sold subject to the condition that it shall not,
by way of trade or otherwise, be lent, re-sold, hired out or
otherwise circulated without the publisher's prior consent
in any form of binding or cover other than that in which it
is published and without a similar condition including this
condition being imposed on the subsequent purchaser.*

British Library Cataloguing in Publication Data

Summerton, Neil
 Noble Task:Eldership and Ministry in the
 Local Church. – 2Rev.ed
 I. Title
 262.15

 ISBN 0 85364 515 9

Typeset by Photoprint, Torquay, Devon
and Printed in Great Britain for The Paternoster Press,
PO Box 300, Carlisle, Cumbria, CA3 0QS
Printed and bound by
The Guernsey Press Co. Ltd, Guernsey, Channel Islands

For
MRS ISOBEL STORDY

CONTENTS

PART B—FULL-TIME CONGREGATIONAL MINISTRY

PREFACE

The preface of any book is the place for excuses and apologies!

This one has its origins in a series of articles which appeared in *Harvester* magazine between October 1984 and November 1985. That will be clear enough to the discerning reader, since in preparing the script for publication in a consolidated form I have for the most part made only rather minor changes. There are two reasons for this. First, the nature of my life as a civil servant, church elder, and husband and father (too often in that order) is such that an extensive revision would probably never be completed. Secondly, encouragement and criticism received in response to the *Harvester* articles from the United States and the Antipodes, as well as from Britain, suggest that, despite my narrow experience and knowledge of the churches, the subject matter answers to real needs and questions in congregations of (Open or Christian) Brethren* origins in a number of places. It therefore seems important to bring the material together as soon as possible, so that it may easily be consulted while it meets a felt need, even if some rough edges remain. The scholar in me finds this deplorable. The administrator reminds me that a timely work which meets much of the requirement (if only it would!) is preferable to a superior piece of work which arrives at the dockside only long after the boat has left!

One consequence is that I have done little to generalize the text to make it immediately applicable to congregations outside the Brethren tradition. But in any case I doubt whether that would have been well advised. For 25 years I have been a member of a Brethren congregation and an elder there for 14 (though I was originally an Anglican, am effectively a strict Baptist when at our

9

house in Suffolk, and some of my best friends are Mennonites, Anglicans, Roman Catholics and Pentecostals!). Insofar as the following chapters carry any conviction, it is in my judgment because they are rooted in that personal experience. To seek to generalize the analysis and application would have the effect, I think, of removing much of the force and authenticity of the text, so that it would seem lifeless and anodyne.

That said, it remains my conviction that the interest being shown in congregational eldership, and in the implications of charismatic gift, in many denominations across the world, is such that there is much that the discerning reader can, with suitable transpositions, apply in their situations from the Brethren experience of eldership. In some circles which I have in mind, the influence of Brethren theology and tradition is so strong (chiefly because so many in leadership there stem originally from Brethren fellowships) that I believe that they would do well to ponder what I have to say, in the hope of avoiding errors of church leadership similar to those into which Brethren congregations have often fallen, especially when the first flush of renewal has passed.

Thanks are due to a considerable number of people. I am grateful to the kindness of Jonathan Lamb, who made the pages of *Harvester* so extensively available for the original articles and who encouraged me to complete the monthly penance which they required. A number of others have encouraged by expressing the hope that the material would be brought into a more permanent form. I should thank especially all who have served with me in eldership of Cholmeley Evangelical Church in Highgate: they will recognize readily the great extent to which this book has grown out of our common experience, and how great is the gap between precept and my own performance as an elder. In addition, discussions with Dr. Kenneth Brownell have been a great stimulus to thought about these matters. John Baigent, Harold Rowdon and Alan Kreider gave much help with the details of further reading—I do not claim to be so well read! My wife, Pauline, and sons, Ian and Matthew, are only too well aware of how much I owe them: it is they who have paid the highest price for this text.

To assert that responsibility for everything included in the text lies with me alone is no less sincere because it is customary. Inevitably, prophecy is imperfect (*1 Corinthians 13:9*). But it is my prayer that this manual bears marks of the prophetic and will accordingly be of use in building up the church (and not simply, as in a few cases of which I have heard, in encouraging good men to stand down from eldership—I suspect from that very fact that it is they who should have stayed and others who should have stood down!).

Highgate, London
June 1986

---

* In what follows, I refer to the denominational connexion by the term by which they are commonly known among Evangelical Christians in the United Kingdom, *viz* 'Brethren'. I do so even though with the passage of time that is becoming less and less satisfactory: many congregations of Brethren origins do not now accept the designation, and informally congregations commonly identify themselves by saying that they 'were Brethren'. This results partly from the disadvantages of being erroneously identified by the ill-informed with the Taylorite Exclusive Brethren, and partly from the very welcome influx to many churches of new Christians who know nothing of their congregation's origins. For the moment, however, such congregations are often much more influenced by their Brethren origins than their members credit.

PREFACE TO THE SECOND EDITION

In preparing a new edition of this book, I have considered carefully how far changes to the earlier text are necessary. Inevitably, with the passage of time and further experience, my own views are changing. So are the Brethren and former Brethren congregations to which the book is primarily addressed, and the wider environment in which each congregation is seeking to be an expression of Christ's body in the world. For the most part, I have however adopted the approach of minimal change, partly because I still substantially agree with what I wrote, and partly because that would again ensure publication sooner rather than later.

Of course, if I were writing from scratch now, some important emphases might be expressed a little differently. If anything, the passage of time has convinced me more than ever of the need for positive, Spirit-filled leadership, seized by a vision from the Lord, for congregations of Brethren origins; and of the need for flexible teams of full-time and part-time supported workers, working closely with people in secular employment, to spearhead the task of church renewal, planting and re-planting, particularly in urban areas. This leadership needs to be coupled with a wide exercise of spiritual gifts across each congregation and a deep experience of the liberty of the Holy Spirit so that those gifts can be exercised to the full for the benefit of the whole body. All this calls for a good deal less caution and fear in some congregations; and a willingness to entrust ourselves to the Lord in the knowledge that he will not take us anywhere that is bad for us (*Luke* 11:11–13).

The concluding sections on further reading and training opportunities have been revised to take account of information available in the autumn of 1993. I am grateful to those concerned with

12

training courses for their patience in sending me up-to-date material; and to John Baigent, Peter Brierley, and Harold Rowdon for their bibliographical help—the section on further reading is now, I freely admit, more their work than mine.

The first edition was sharply criticised by some for sexist language and the failure to address head-on the question of whether women can be elders. To some extent, the former blemish derives from the absence from English of pronouns in common gender, and from my assumption that most people would be prepared to accept my exhortation to regard the use of the male pronoun as including the female, without any derogatory inference as to the status of the latter. This was a clear error, and I have sought to correct it wherever it can be done without too clumsy a result: frequently I have had to use the third person plural in a singular sense (I abhor the modern 'he/she'!). I have done this to avoid giving offence and to try to head off mistaken assumptions about my attitude to the exercise of gift by women. Further, I have concluded that I could not possibly allow a book to be published on leadership and ministry in the local church in 1994 without including material on the ministry and leadership of women. In doing so, I hope that I have not strained the shape of the original work too much—I have concluded that the best course is an additional appendix specifically on the subject. It is too much to hope that all will agree with my conclusions—on both flanks! It will be clear that I continue to struggle with the theology of headship, but am more and more convinced on grounds of scripture and experience that the ministry of women has been scandalously curtailed during much of the history of the church to its serious detriment. On the authority of the Lord a bad tree cannot bring forth good fruit. So in determining the theological question, weight must be given to the evident blessing which the Lord pours out on the ministry of women.

Highgate, London
December, 1993

THE NEED FOR EFFECTIVE ELDERSHIP

One of the characteristics of the Protestant Reformation has been to spawn a wide variety of sects[1] and denominations, nowhere more so than in the Anglo-Saxon world. In origin at least, those bodies share a common corpus of fundamental Christian truth based upon the supremacy of scripture. Sects are marked out from denominations by the belief in greater or lesser degree that they have each, to the exclusion of all others, become the sole vehicle of that truth. Otherwise the matters which distinguish one Christian sect or denomination from another are their characteristic beliefs and practices on items which, though sometimes important both objectively or in their own eyes, do not usually trench on the bedrock of the faith.

Though it now has rivals, there have among the major bodies been few more distinctive than the Brethren, both of the open and narrower varieties. That distinctiveness has been derived partly from a distinctive framework for interpreting scripture—though it was in fact more widely adopted among Evangelicals than is often supposed.[2] That resulted in a distinctive mental culture.

But as important in identifying the Brethren as a denomination were certain *principles* and *practices* of church life. Their particular configuration was important in identifying a congregation as an 'assembly'. But it is interesting how few of them, taken individually, are unique to the Brethren. Certainly not the independency of the local church—though few denominations have taken the principle

1. I refer to Christian, not heretical sects.
2. See Ernest R. Sandeen, *The Roots of Fundamentalism: British and American Millennarianism, 1800–1930* (Chicago and London: The University of Chicago Press, 1970).

to such absurd extremes. Certainly not belief in scripture as the final authority in faith and practice. Certainly not believer's baptism. Nor the limitations on the exercise of the ministry of women, nor the requirement for head-covering. Nor strict, nor open, communion. In the last analysis, *the* distinctive features are no more than two: the particular form, spiritual character and content of worship at the Lord's Table; and the particular manifestation of plural government and leadership of the local congregation—in the usual shorthand, eldership or oversight.

Reference to government and leadership, as distinct from pattern of ministry, is deliberate. To suggest that the Brethren are unique in their emphasis on plural *ministry* in the local congregation would be to make too great an historical claim. For a millennium or so, the church in western Europe has tended to think in terms of a single full-time paid priest or minister to each congregation, to whom has fallen the duty of discharging most, if not all, the spiritual ministries in that congregation. This model of ministry has deeply influenced the western European understanding. Thanks to the importance of western Europe in the missionary movements of the sixteenth century (Catholic) and the nineteenth and twentieth centuries (Protestant), the model has been exported to many other places. Today, it may be argued, it is reinforced by the dominance of the presidential or chief executive model of leadership in political and business affairs in the West — notwithstanding interest in some management circles in shared leadership.

Monarchical *government* of the church emerged early in its history, with the recognition in the second and third centuries of single governing elders (or bishops) in the cities of the Empire. But it may be surmised that the dominance of the monarchical model of *ministry* was given strong encouragement by the comparatively late adoption in the west of the territorial system of parishes— possibly as much for the practical reason of securing a good and equitable coverage of ministry as for theological reasons relating to the special position of the priesthood.

Nevertheless, throughout the history of the church, generally in association with spiritual revival, the principle of plural or group ministry has always tended to reassert itself. It may readily be seen since the Reformation in groups such as the Anabaptists, the Pietists, the Moravians, the Methodists, and others emerging from the first and second Evangelical revivals. But it was by no means the invention or discovery of the Reformation. The same process can be discerned in the dissenting groups of the middle ages—the

Lollards, the Hussites and the Waldenses, for example. It can also be seen in the spiritual movements which were contained within the western Catholic church, for example, in the mendicant orders and in the collegial spirituality and missionary endeavour of the monasteries (demonstrating incidentally that there was no necessary causal relation between the ideas of sacerdotalism and monarchical leadership in the church).

So, turning to the Brethren, it is arguable that the truly distinctive feature has not been the plural *ministry* of the elders—in any case, the best of the tradition has never regarded that as being confined to the elders—but their collective *government* and *leadership* of the congregation.

There is no doubt that Brethren churches in Britain—and it seems elsewhere in the world—are suffering from a crisis of identity and purpose[3] which is exacerbated by the fact that other groups which are experimenting with similar approaches to ministry seem to be enjoying great spiritual blessing. This book is premised on the belief that the spiritual state of many congregations (of which the crisis of identity and purpose is no more than a symptom) can be traced to deficiencies in government, leadership and ministry—in a phrase, to widespread default in the practice of eldership.

It is in the nature of distinctive principles and practices that they become hallowed traditions which give meaning to the group when other sources of vitality have been exhausted. At the same time they limit the possibilities of new understandings and practices. A passionate belief in the *principle* of plural government, leadership and ministry in the church is not enough for spiritual growth. There is moreover a real danger that the conviction that Brethren ecclesiology is scripturally well nigh perfect can bring about an atrophy of thought, in particular about *how* eldership is to be *practised* individually, and about *how* corporate government and leadership are to be made effective in practice. It is always dangerous to believe that one is right; it is frequently the step precedent to ceasing to understand the workings of the precept concerned. And the evidence of scripture is that God is rather little interested in adherence to principle when it is not accompanied by effective practice and spiritual experience. The evidence from many denominations is that soundness on plural government,

---

3. Harold H. Rowdon, *Who are the Brethren and does it matter?*, (Exeter: The Paternoster Press for the Christian Brethren Research Fellowship, 1986). Though circumstances are changing somewhat in the UK in 1993, these concerns are if anything more marked in many other places.

ministry and leadership is unimportant to enjoying God's blessing. He blesses where he finds longing for that blessing, not theoretical perfection of church order; and where he finds spiritual ministry and leadership being exercised—irrespective of the institutional form in which they are cast.

That is not to say, however, that patterns of church order which are at odds with the *principles* (not the details) outlined in scripture do not constrain effectiveness in building up the local congregation into something approaching the biblical model. What follows is based on the continuing belief that the New Testament practice was the government and leadership of the local congregation by a number of elder-overseers (shepherds), sometimes in collaboration for periods with a church planter or a church-planting team, and that this is too wise a practice to be abandoned or to be allowed to fall into disrepute through unthinking adulation. It is taken for granted that the practice continues to be worth following.

The aim is therefore to look closely at the principles and practice of plural eldership; to re-evaluate those principles in the light of scripture and today's conditions; and to suggest ways in which the performance of individual elders, and of elderships as groups, may be improved to the benefit of the congregations for which they are responsible. Throughout, the aim is to stimulate further discussion of these vital matters and to consider the practical (the 'how' of eldership) as well as the underlying principles.

Unashamedly, the intention is to sketch the outlines of a manual of eldership, though because of my own rather narrow experience I do not claim the results as being in any sense definitive. While it addresses itself particularly to the Brethren tradition, it is my hope that the suggestions made may be of use to those experimenting with plural eldership in denominations as various as evangelical Anglicans and strict Baptists; and to those like the new churches and many Pentecostals to whom it is the normal form of church leadership.

In outline, the book first considers who should be elders and how they should be selected. In a number of subsequent chapters it examines the various tasks of the elder in some detail. Then, it turns to the crucial matters of the relationships implied in eldership, i.e., between elders, with the deacons and others in positions of responsibility, and with the rest of the congregation. Part A concludes by looking at the training and development of elders.

Part B considers some important questions relating to the integration of full-time Christian ministries into congregations with a strong tradition of plural leadership and charismatic ministry. This is a matter of continuing interest and concern in Brethren churches in Britain and elsewhere, because of the extensive experiments now being made. It is important that wherever the move is made it should be beneficial rather than disturbing for the churches. The lessons to be drawn from Part B may also be of value to churches of other traditions where the norm has been monarchical ministry, but which are developing 'lay' eldership or team ministries. Some of the issues addressed tend to arise wherever fallen human beings (even Spirit-filled ones) seek to work together in groups, and wherever congregations experiment with a wider view of leadership and ministry than has been customary.

PART A

Principles and Practice
of Congregational Eldership

I

The Calling to Eldership

1

QUALIFICATIONS FOR ELDERSHIP

It ought to go without saying that no one should be asked, or attempt, to undertake the onerous responsibilities of congregational eldership if they do not have the necessary qualifications to discharge them. The New Testament is unequivocal that effective ministry derives, in the power of the Holy Spirit, from character, capacities, attitudes, approach and spiritual gift and not from any other source. Accordingly, the pastoral epistles are anxious to establish above all that the right kind of people are recognized as elders. It is important, however, that in assessing qualifications for eldership, there should be a sufficiently broad understanding of all the various qualities and gifts needed if elders are to carry out their tasks with competence. Too narrow an approach can result in the calling of people who are, at best, only partially equipped and who are not fully able to bear the burdens of eldership.

Personal qualifications

A large proportion (but not all) of the passages in the New Testament which refer to eldership focus on the personal qualities required in the elder (see in particular 1 Timothy 3:1–7 and Titus 1:6–9). There can be no doubt that this emphasis is deliberate and that we are intended to infer that the qualities listed are indispensable. In the absence of those qualities no amount of title, formal supporting structures, recognition, ordination, long service, or even spiritual gifts can enable the individual to exercise effectively

---

* Scripture quotations are from the Revised Standard Version unless otherwise stated.

and beneficially spiritual ministries which will build up the congregation.

In some circles, much time and energy has been expended in disputing details, such as whether the requirement that the elder should be 'the husband of one wife' (*1 Timothy* 3:2) implies the exclusion of the unmarried from eldership. That does not sit well with the suggestion of both the Lord and Paul that singleness can be advantageous for Christian ministry (*Matthew 19:12; 1 Corinthians 7:25ff.*), and the probability is that the particular requirement intends only to exclude the divorced and the sexually immoral. But this is to focus on one particular aspect of the relevant passages (in a rather eccentric manner), with the result that the central message is distorted and obscured—a favourite method employed by Satan to distract attention from the real burden of scripture.

Happily, the rest of the guidance on the personal qualities required is beyond contention or misunderstanding. It is significant that it concentrates on observable matters of character and conduct, on the works which are the practical evidence of a living faith (*James 2:8–26*). The implication is that the elder should be selected only on the basis of careful and lengthy scrutiny of the individual's life (*1 Timothy 5:24–25*). Taken with Peter's remarks in *1 Peter 5*, the passages in *1 Timothy* and *Titus* may be summarized as demanding in the elder the following:[1*]

* *deep spirituality*: this must be shown in devotion to God, in love for what is good, in goodness itself, in holiness, in humility (*1 Timothy 3:6; Titus 1:7–8, 1 Peter 5:6*), and in right ordering of priorities between material, social and spiritual objectives;
* *spiritual maturity*: the elder is not to be a novice in the faith, but must have a full and balanced grasp of Christian teaching (*1 Timothy 3:6*);
* *emotional stability*: the candidate is not to be violent, quarrelsome, or quick-tempered, but sensible, dignified and gentle (*1 Timothy 3:2–3; Titus 1:7*);
* *personal discipline*: this group of qualities is closely related to the preceding group, but the requirement of self-control, perseverance and soberness (specifically with respect to alcohol) implies an ability to discipline time and body so as to achieve personal and group goals (*1 Timothy 3:2–3; 2 Timothy 4:1–5; and Titus 1:7–8*);
* *sexual probity*: the essence of the requirement that the elder must

---

* Footnotes will be found at the end of each chapter.

be the 'husband of one wife' (*1 Timothy 3:2*) is that they must be beyond reproach in their sexual relationships; since many pastoral problems concern sexual matters and relationships with spouses and children, it is obviously important that the elder should be blameless in these things;

* *competence managerially and in personal relations*: the quality of the prospective elder's relationships with spouse and children has a positive as well as a negative aspect; responsibility in the congregation requires a subtle blend of love, guidance, counsel and authority, and these are just the qualities required to lead an extended household (*1 Timothy 3:5–6; Titus 1:6*);
* *practical generosity*: elder and spouse are to be generous in their use of their funds, home and goods, and must have their material priorities right (*1 Timothy 3:2–3*);
* *social approval*: within the congregation, the person suitable to be an elder will be known to be blameless and above reproach, and in wider society is to be held in good reputation—unbelievers are often remarkably perceptive of the shortcomings of Christians, especially by way of lack of integrity and cant (*1 Timothy 3:2, 7*).

Much of this is well known, but sometimes only in rather a superficial sense. Despite the insistence of the pastoral epistles that these multiple and diverse personal qualities are *essential* in anybody who is to be called to eldership, it is striking how often churches of all kinds succeed in honouring these requirements in the breach. Accordingly, elders are often selected because they are senior in years, they have done much good work in other positions in the congregation, they are spiritually admirable, or simply because there are vacancies which, it is thought, must be filled.

This last factor should be strenuously resisted. There is no rule, and should be none, requiring a congregation to have such and such a number of elders, even if people with the requisite qualifications are not available. It may be that smaller congregations will often turn out to have only one member suitable to be an elder. In such cases, the principle of plurality should not be turned into a fetish. In many congregations it would be a major step forward to take the requirements of the New Testament with deadly seriousness and to appoint *only* those meeting them. Those without the necessary personal qualities cannot be expected suddenly to acquire them on appointment—though if they have them, the exercise of office will develop and mature them. When the wrong people are appointed, the congregation concerned can expect to

have many a long year in which to rue the consequences of its lack
of spiritual discernment in its choice of elders.

Functional Qualifications

The possession of these daunting personal qualities is an *essential*
qualification for eldership. But the possession of them in some
degree is not *sufficient of itself* to qualify a person to be an elder. It
may be argued that Paul's purpose in the pastoral epistles was to
lay down certain indispensable requirements, to prevent Timothy
and Titus from appointing those who could not begin to discharge
the role and tasks of the elder because they were personally
unsuitable. But digging beneath the surface of the personal
qualities needed, we can see that some of them are proposed as
indicating competence to discharge the *functions* of eldership. For
example, 1 *Timothy 3:5* is explicit that the ability to manage family
and the domestic household indicates the possession of competence
in pastoring, disciplining and managing the congregation.

It is moreover important to give due weight not simply to those
texts which itemize the personal qualities of elders, but also to the
context of those passages in the pastoral epistles, and to the other
material in *The Acts of the Apostles* (notably *Acts 20: 17–35*) and 1 *and
2 Corinthians* which deal either directly or by implication with the
tasks of the elder. Qualification for eldership needs to be considered
in the light of those tasks as well as the personal qualifications
required.

The tasks of eldership will be considered in detail in later
chapters. Suffice it to say now that the New Testament sees elders
as taking responsibility as the pastoral leaders of the congregation.
Central to that are the functional tasks of pastoring and teaching—
the elders are nothing if they are not the principal pastor-teachers
of the flock. Those who do not have the necessary spiritual gifts for
these prime tasks ought not to be called as elders: and the spiritual
gifts which should be particularly sought are those of pastor-and-
teacher (*Ephesians 4:11*), prophet (*ibid.; 1 Corinthians 12 and 14*),
utterance of wisdom, utterance of knowledge, and the discernment
of spirits (the latter three being of special relevance to pastoral care
and discipline). Hence to both Timothy and Titus, Paul is crystal
clear that the indispensable quality, which incidentally distinguishes the elder from the deacon, is the ability to master Christian
doctrine, to evaluate it in others, to teach it, and to debate it with
those who teach falsehood. (*1 Timothy 3:2; Titus 1:9–16*).[2]

The pastor-teacher ministry is also one of the principal means by which the elders' leadership and vision is communicated to the congregation, and the ability to communicate is one of the key requirements of effective leadership.

There may well be those who are inclined to rebel against this emphasis and to argue that elders need more practical gifts in order to ensure that their administration is smooth and efficient. In answer, it may be said, first, that this mistakes the emphasis which both Old and New Testaments place on the need for the flock of God to be led by shepherds who will ensure that it is fed spiritually. For this purpose soundness of character needs to be brought together with the reception and transmission of the word of the Lord as the means of feeding, protecting and restoring individual members of the flock. This ministry does not necessarily have to be exercised from the platform and the centre of gravity of the gifts of one elder may be towards teaching while that of another may be towards pastoring. But all need a sound grasp of the Faith and the ability to teach and instruct in small groups and one-to-one in the pastoral situation.

Secondly, if elders lack practical skill in such administration as is necessary in the flock, let them appoint a person or persons (perhaps as deacons if they have the high spiritual qualities also demanded for that office) to assist them. Moreover, in an eldership of any size one or more of the body may be able to discharge these tasks so long as they do not prevent them from giving priority to the overseeing tasks. But at all costs the error of appointing those who lack either the character and spiritual qualities, or eldership gifts, or both, should be avoided.

Practical qualifications

There is however a more mundane qualification which is essential if someone is to be called to be an elder. It is the willingness and *opportunity* to devote time and energy to the task. It requires great personal commitment, and a readiness to make eldership a priority in Christian service. The demands of personal and group prayer, of meeting in oversight, of preparation for teaching, of pastoral visitation, and of giving necessary leadership and guidance to congregational activities are inevitably very great. A particular individual may have the character and gifts, and even the inclination, to be an elder, but may not have the time.

The reasons may be various: the individual's daily job may be too demanding; existing commitments in other Christian service within or outside the congregation may be too great; job or Christian service may take the prospective candidate from home too frequently and for too long periods. Or demands and pressures of bringing up a young family may be such that the individual ought not to devote at that stage of life the time required for eldership—my own experience has led me to doubt whether churches ought to call to eldership those who have both a full-time job outside the church and the responsibilities of a young family. (The requirement that the elder's children should be believers implies in itself a certain maturity in years (*Titus 1:6*).) There may, too, be implications at the other end of the age spectrum: there may come a moment when age and infirmity make it impossible to meet the demands of active eldership.

The demands upon time and emotional energy inherent in eldership impinge particularly upon the marriage relationship. The demands on the elder's partner are direct as well as indirect: for elder and partner are required to make their home available to the congregation and that inevitably makes direct demands upon the partner. This implies, for example, that the elder's spouse, just as much as the elder, must wholeheartedly concur in and embrace their partner's calling to eldership, and be willing to share in those tasks of eldership which have to be discharged by the couple together.

In the absence of a shared commitment and calling in this sense, there can be real dangers. If the sacrifice demanded of the elder is not gladly accepted by the marriage partner, serious strains can be imposed on the marriage and regrettably it is not uncommon for marriages to break down altogether in Christian service in the absence of such joint commitment. In some cases, this problem, and the sacrifice which the elder's spouse is called upon to make, is all the greater because of the limbo into which they can be assigned, presumably out of fear that, as can sometimes happen, they will come to dominate the church as the power behind the throne.

If these are the desiderata of elders, by what particular processes should they be selected and in what circumstances should they retire? It is one thing to have in the congregation those who *ought* to be elders; it is another to succeed in calling them to the office. It is to these questions that the next chapter turns.

1. For more extended discussions of qualifications for eldership, see Bruce Stabbert, *The Team Concept: Paul's church leadership patterns or ours?* (Tacoma, Washington: Hegg Bros. 1982) pp. 129–140; A. Kuen, *Ministères dans l'église* (St. Legier: Editions

Emmaüs, 1983) pp. 101–109; and Alexander Strauch, *Biblical Eldership: An urgent call to restore Biblical Church leadership*, (Littleton, Col.: Lewis and Roth, 1986), pp. 75–89 and 215–234.

2. Elsewhere I have suggested a tentative scheme associating the spiritual gifts listed in *Romans 12, 1 Corinthians 12–14*, and *Ephesians 4* with the various functional tasks of elders and deacons, viz:

Functional tasks	*Relevant spiritual gifts*
Pastoral	Pastor; utterance of wisdom; utterance of knowledge; discernment
Teaching	Prophet; teacher; exhortation; utterance of wisdom; utterance of knowledge
Leadership, particularly strategic guidance	Apostle; prophet; administrator (*lit.* 'steersman'); faith; leader
Government, regulation and discipline	Utterance of wisdom; utterance of knowledge; discernment; ability to distinguish spirits; ? interpretation; ruler
Diaconal	Service; contribution; acts of mercy; giving aid; helpers

See N. W. Summerton, 'Leadership and Ministry in the Church', in CBRF Journal No. 30 (*Leadership in the Churches* (London: CBRF, 1980), p. 30).

2

APPOINTMENT, RECOGNITION
AND RETIREMENT

It is all too common to hear church members and full-time Christian workers lamenting with a mixture of guilt, sorrow, and anger that their congregation appears to be in the hands of those who are unsuitable to be elders and yet who show no sign of withdrawing from office. Such remarks imply on the one hand that the member has some idea of what an elder ought to be and do, and on the other that in the church concerned there may be something wrong with the process of selection and with the elders' conception of the nature of eldership.

Choosing elders

There is in the churches of Brethren background a wide variety in the processes of choosing elders. Some churches, particularly small ones, do not have elders, the conduct of the church being in the hands of a business meeting of the male members or possibly of all the members. In others, each elder is in effect self-selected, in that it is announced that there is to be a meeting of brethren in oversight and that those brethren who consider that they are entitled to attend are welcome to do so. Under this arrangement, there is likely to be a tension between the nerve of the person who feels that he might attend and the mechanisms of social control at the disposal of the existing membership who will probably make it clear enough who in their opinion ought to attend. Such an arrangement seems likely to ensure that those most suited to be elders will not attend; and regrettably it suggests that eldership inheres only in transacting business at the oversight meeting.

Where the existing body succeeds in making it clear who should attend, the arrangement verges on the norm in Brethren assemblies, viz. the selection of new appointees by the existing body of elders. In one congregation of Brethren background of which I have been told, however, the elders were initially selected by inviting each church member to nominate those whom they regarded as suited to be elders and the resulting body submit themselves to a repetition of the process each year.[1]

Other churches in the process of introducing elders are as likely as not to follow the usual selection practices of their tradition, or to accept the nominations of the full-time leader who is introducing the change.

In the light of this variation of practice, it is worth referring to the pattern followed by the churches described in the New Testament. The evidence is that there were from the earliest days in each locality individuals who were described as elder (presbyter)-shepherds (overseers). This description marked out those who bore it from the rest of the congregation for whom they had pastoral responsibility. Thus Paul writes to 'all the saints in Christ Jesus which are at Philippi, *with* the elders and deacons' (*Colossians* 1:1); and passing through Miletus he calls to him a distinct body, the elders of the church at Ephesus (*Acts 20:17*), and instructs them in their pastoral tasks. Nor would there be any point in Paul's advising Titus whom to 'appoint' as elders 'in every town' (*Titus* 1:5) if there were not a distinct office to be filled and the *locus classicus* of the elder's attributes refers specifically to such an office (*1 Timothy 3:1*).

This much seems clear. But the method of selection in the early church is more controversial. In addressing the elders of Ephesus, Paul said that it was the Holy Spirit who had made them guardians of the flock (*Acts 20:28*). We shall see in a moment how important this requirement is: it should go without saying that anyone appointed to any role in any church ought to be the choice of the Holy Spirit; an appointment of the flesh is bound to be without benefit to the congregation, if not a positive hindrance. But it is possible to draw the wrong inference from the principle: for unless we take the view that the elder is self-selecting under the direct guidance of the Holy Spirit, a proposition which is not consistent with the New Testament practice, it follows that there must be an instrument of the necessary revelation. The vacant place among the Twelve was filled by the Jewish practice of casting lots (*Acts* 1:24–26) and the disciples clearly saw this as the means by which the divine choice was revealed. There is no record of the repetition of the practice after Pentecost, however. The direct references in the New Testament to the appointment of elders are universally to their selection by the apostles or their assistants, as for example when Paul and Barnabas on their first missionary journey 'appointed elders . . . in every church' (*Acts 14:23*). But the selection of the Seven (as deacons perhaps) was by choice of 'the whole multitude' (*Acts 6:5*); and the selection of Paul and Barnabas for missionary work was by the prophets and teachers, i.e. the leaders, of the church at Antioch (*Acts 13:1–3*).

So if there is a norm for the appointment of elders in the New Testament, it is by itinerating church planters and the only instance which approximates to present-day Brethren practice of appointment by the existing elders (*Acts 13:1–3*) does not directly refer to the appointment of elders. We do not however know how elders were appointed, for example, in the Jerusalem church or in established congregations already under the rule of the elders appointed by the apostles. Perhaps the variety of the New Testament practice in appointment to office or task may be taken as indicating the scope for varying the practice according to circumstances, and for allowing those with an interchurch role, the elders, and the congregation as a whole, to share in differing degrees in the process of selection. Certainly it is the case that church elders would often do well on a number of matters both to take the congregation into their confidence and to call on the advice of godly outsiders, rather than to wrestle with matters on their own.

It is characteristic of Technological Man of the twentieth century to worry abnormally about the precise mechanism of selection. But biblically of much greater importance is its manner and spirit. Be we ever so precise about the *modus operandi*, it will be of no avail if the mechanism still succeeds in choosing the wrong people. For this reason it may not matter much whether selection of elders is by church planters, the existing elders, or the congregation as a whole, so long as all are certain that the outcome is the choice of God.

The unambiguous testimony of the New Testament is that selection for any Christian ministry should be undertaken carefully, prayerfully, sacrificially, and with prophetic witness. It is a general principle that we should not be hasty in the laying on of hands (*1 Timothy 5:22*) and it should be taken with special seriousness in the selection of elders: choose in haste and the existing elders and the congregation may well repent at leisure! Ignoring the comma in the Revised Standard Version, Howard Marshall takes the prayer and fasting of *Acts 14:23* as related to the appointment of elders and, like F. F. Bruce, compares the words with the circumstances of

Paul's and Barnabas's own selection for missionary service:[2] it was
with worship and fasting that the call was made known (*Acts 13:2*)
and with prayer and fasting that the church commended them to
the work (*Acts 13:3*). The call was made known by prophetic
utterance ('The Holy Spirit said, . . .'); and Timothy's selection for
ministry was similarly revealed by prophetic utterance in a gathering composed of at least one apostle and the elders (1 *Timothy 4:14*
and 2 *Timothy 1:8*).

We can deduce from this that selection for eldership is not
something to be done casually in a few minutes in an elders'
business committee as if we were selecting the secretary of the Golf
Club, but as those charged with the responsibility of selection wait
sacrificially upon the Lord for his guidance in worship and prayer.
In this, the procedure by which the college of cardinals elect a new
pope in conclave is perhaps more faithful to the biblical tradition
than many a Brethren oversight!

With this accent on revelation to the church of who should
undertake ministry, it ought to follow that there should be no
difficulty about the congregation's recognizing with unanimity
those who are chosen. Secondly, the views of the individual
scarcely seem to enter into the process. It is to be expected that
the recognition of the divine word would be shared, or at least
accepted, by the individual concerned and, as a matter of common
sense, if the individual rejects the call there is little that the
congregation can do, though in due course it may be the poorer
because of that rejection.

Recognition of elders

The New Testament refers extensively to a further practice related
to selection for ministry—the laying on of hands. It is widely
neglected in Brethren churches, possibly because it is regarded as
having ecclesiastical taint; and in other groups it tends to be given an
unjustifiably narrow ambit—to set aside special individuals to one
particular sort of ministry. In the New Testament it was in fact
widely used to initiate individuals to every kind of ministry, for
example, the commendation of Paul and Barnabas to missionary
work, Timothy's selection as a teacher, and the commissioning of
the Seven by the apostles in *Acts 6:6*. It is scarcely credible that it
was not also practised when elders were appointed, especially as it
was ordinary practice in appointing members of the Sanhedrin.[3]

The laying on of hands had a two-fold function: first, as
conferring and reinforcing the spiritual gifts required for the

particular ministry (Timothy's gift was given him by prophetic utterance when Paul and the elders laid their hands on him—*1 Timothy 4:14; 2 Timothy 1:6*). This emphasis challenges the commonly-held notion that selection as an elder entails no more than acknowledging those who are already doing the work of an elder, with the implication that it does not really matter whether they are recognized as elders or not. It is true that in the prayerful consideration of candidates the search should concentrate on those who manifest the gifts relevant to eldership, who are already using them in considerable degree, and who show the commitment to the life of the congregation that is required. But the call to eldership implies a greater change of position, role and task than is supposed by the catch-words that we simply acknowledge those who are doing the work of an elder.

Secondly, it may reasonably be inferred, for example from *Acts 6:6* and *13:3*, that the laying on of hands was an act at which the whole church was present.[4] In this way the whole church was associated both with the conferring of the authority for the task and commendation to it. This was a secondary purpose of the laying on of hands, but it is nevertheless important that any ministry in the church, and particularly that of the elder, should be properly recognized by the whole congregation. Even in a military formation, where the structure and sanctions of authority are quite different from those of a church, leadership and authority cannot be exercised properly unless the leader is recognized and accepted by those who are led. So too in the church a ministry cannot be fully effective unless it is recognized and accepted by the congregation and each individual member. The laying on of hands by the elders on behalf of and before the congregation publicly confers that recognition and acceptance, even if subsequently only the manner and nature of the elder's service of the church can justify and maintain that recognition.

It is essential that elders should know that they enjoy, and continue to enjoy, the confidence of the church as a whole. There is deep encouragement in meeting in prayer and worship to inaugurate a ministry. In the case of Brethren churches, it has long been done for missionaries and other full-time workers; it is curious that it should not be done in respect of elders who bear such a heavy responsibility for the home congregations.

Retirement from eldership

The need to retain the confidence of the congregation leads

conveniently to the vexed question of withdrawal from eldership.
The Brethren tradition is, once an elder, always an elder: only
removal to another church, death, total mental or physical
incapacity, rank heresy and immorality are seen as reasons for
withdrawal. It is a tradition which has damaged many churches
and stems from the tendency to see eldership as a status rather
than a responsibility, a distinction on which more will be said in
the next chapter.

All the things just noted are reasons for withdrawal or removal
from office. But eldership requires not only spiritual qualifications
but also opportunity and ability to perform the tasks and duties of
eldership. Qualifications may be removed only by death, or gross
error or sin. But more mundane considerations affect opportunity
and ability. The Lord may call an elder to a wider Christian service,
either temporarily or permanently, which is incompatible with
effective discharge of the burden of eldership. Or opportunity may
be prevented by chronic ill-health, declining energy, or moderate
loss of faculties. It may be even that the individual ought simply to
make way for others with greater gift for the office.

Sometimes, the individual concerned, especially if they remain
devoted to the Lord's work, may not recognize the situation. Each
elder should monitor their own circumstances and performance.
But just as initial selection is not the responsibility of the individual,
so the elders as a body should not be afraid in love to break the
news to an elder that the time has come to lay down the burden,
and when that call is made it ought to be respected just as the
initial call was accepted as the Lord's will. If the elders do not grasp
this nettle, members of the church may do so with less satisfactory
consequences!

In view of the emphasis on seeking the Lord's mind in selection
it would be inappropriate to lay down hard and fast rules that an
elder should serve only for a limited period of years, or that
retirement should be automatic at, say, 70 years of age. But the
eldership should discipline itself to maintain a regular review both
of its existing membership and of the need to call additional elders,
and it is worth considering whether appointment should be
explicitly for, say, 5 years with provision for reappointment.
Wise elders, whatever their age but particularly after the age of 70,
will regard their positions as continually at the Lord's disposal via
their colleagues and the church as a whole.

It need not follow from this that the elder who stands down
must lose status in the church, a factor which often regrettably
keeps people from retiring even when they have long known that

their time has come. It is questionable whether anyone who prizes the status of eldership rather than the temporary opportunity to be the servant of the church is suitable to become or remain an elder. But there is no reason why the congregation should not continue to give proper honour to those who have served it long and well, even though they have rightly laid down their responsibilities. One possibility is to give those who have retired the title of 'elder emeritus' so long as it is understood that they no longer bear the responsibility of oversight of the flock.

---

1. For a more extended analysis of different types of church government in Brethren assemblies, see Brian Mills, 'Leadership in the Churches' in the Christian Brethren Research Fellowship Journal No. 30, *Leadership in the Churches* (London: CBRF, 1980) pp. 48–52.

2. I. Howard Marshall, *The Acts of the Apostles: An Introduction and Commentary* (Leicester: The Inter-Varsity Press, 1980) p. 241; F. F. Bruce, *The Acts of the Apostles: The Greek Text with Introduction and Commentary* (Leicester: The Inter-Varsity Press, 2nd edition, 1952) p. 286.

3. See F. F. Bruce, *op. cit.*, p. 154; and I. Howard Marshall, *op. cit.*, p. 127.

4. See F. F. Bruce, *op. cit.*, p. 254.

II

The Office and Tasks of the Elder

3

THE FIVE-FOLD TASK

Already, there has been frequent reference to the *office* and *tasks* of eldership, in order to give a necessary perspective to the questions of identifying and recognizing elders. It is time now to examine the office and task more closely as a preparation for detailed discussion of each of the functional components of the task.

Office, not status

In discussing the process of selecting elders, it was noted that the New Testament conceives of a distinct *office* of elder. This concept presents a fundamental challenge to a view frequently encountered in Brethren churches and in other groups which wish to emphasise the priesthood and ministry of all believers. It has important implications for an understanding of the tasks of the elder, namely, what the elder is expected to *do* in the congregation.

The challenge lies in the opinion, widely held among the Brethren, either consciously from scripture or unconsciously, that eldership is *no more than a status* in the congregation which is conferred as a result of the spiritual experience and qualifications, or simply the age, of the person concerned. In this understanding, eldership is the equivalent of an honour awarded for virtue or long service.

This view can have serious consequences for the individual's ministry as an elder and for the congregation. Put bluntly, it makes for armchair elders. As a result, the office is frequently sought for the prestige which it gives. This is all the more serious if the individual concerned feels that they have achieved little or no status in any other aspect of their life, so that the limited community of the church becomes the sole arena in which they may secure the recognition which they value. In numerous places in the gospels however, we find Jesus counselling his followers against concern for position. His rejection of desire for it was devastating: 'let the greatest among you become as the youngest,[1] and the leader as one who serves' (*Luke 22:26*).

The second consequence of this view is a failure to perceive that becoming an elder entails a change in the individual's role and function in the congregation. In the absence of this perception, the elder concerned may simply continue with such ministry as was previously exercised within, or often mainly outside, the congregation, and may feel no need to reflect deeply in the light of scripture on what is now required. Further, when the prestige of eldership is the chief focus of a person's thoughts, it is to be expected that they will not readily withdraw from the position for age or other reason, any more than the person who has received an honour expects to have to relinquish it.

When eldership is viewed as an office or responsibility, a number of important general implications can be discerned, which form a framework within which to consider the individual tasks of eldership.

First, office implies at once *authority* and *accountability*. Nowhere were these twin and opposing concepts expressed more concisely than in the remark of the centurion to Jesus that he was a man under authority with soldiers under him (*Matthew 8:8*). Unquestionably, the elder is entitled to exercise authority in the congregation (but not to lord or domineer over it—*Luke 22:25; 1 Peter 5:3*); this authority is ultimately to be seen in the right to exercise pastoral discipline. The congregation is for its part required to submit to that authority when duly and properly exercised (e.g., *1 Peter 5:5*). With authority goes the right and responsibility of leadership, on which more will be said in a moment. On the other hand, the exercise of authority is, as in the case of the centurion, vicarious: the elder is an under-shepherd whose ministry is derived from the Chief Shepherd. In consequence, there rests on the leader a heavy requirement of constant and final accountability to God for the discharge of the tasks.

More important, however, is that office implies not privilege or right, but *duty* and *obligation*. In the Graeco-Roman world, the word had that connotation, as in the case of the centurion. But in the New Testament it is given a unique intensity in respect of the Christian leader, including the elder (see *1 Peter 5:2–5*). Elders are called upon to set aside status and to give themselves in sacrificial service, just as Jesus did himself (see *Philippians 2:5–6*): 'Let the leader [become] as one who serves' (*Luke 22:26*); 'whoever would be great among you must be your servant, and whoever would be first among you must be slave of all' (*Mark 10:43–44*). Privilege and right are to be rejected in favour of table-waiting to the point of laying down life. In this, the servant is not greater than the Master, for Mark records that Jesus went on to say, 'For the Son of man . . . came not to be served but to serve, and to give his life a ransom for many.' (*v.45*—see also *Philippians 2:8*.)

The requisite attitude of mind was illustrated with poignant power when the Master washed the feet of those who had learned from him (*John 13:4–17*), and who were in turn to lead the nascent church. It is an illustration which needs to be read in conjunction with Jesus's translation of the servants of *John 13:16* (who were not greater than their master) into his friends for whom he was to lay down his life (*John 15:13–15*). Paradoxically, nothing sheds more light on the *status* attaching to the office of elder: those over whom the elder exercises (real) authority are to be regarded not as servants but as friends whom the elder serves in the humblest respects, and for whom he is prepared to sacrifice himself in costly service. Like the pope, the elder's title is servant of the servants of God!

A five-fold task

There is a tendency in Brethren thought to confuse eldership and diaconal tasks. But the position is worse than that. It is common to hear the lament that elders spend much of their time discussing practical details of buildings, finance, furnishing, transport and other arrangements which, it may be argued, lie outside the biblical definition of the task of the deacon, let alone that of the elder. The temptation often seems to be to reverse completely the biblical order and priorities.

The following chapters are based on the view that the elder has a task comprising five intertwined, inter-connected and mutually reinforcing strands, viz:

(1) pastoring the flock;
(2) teaching the flock;
(3) ordering the flock, i.e., all that relates to initiation, admission, discipline, and *in extremis* withdrawal of fellowship;
(4) steering, encouraging and enabling the flock, i.e., leading it; and

(5)   prayer, especially for the flock.

It will readily be seen that not all these components are of the same nature. In essence, the first three constitute the principal instruments for fashioning the fourth strand. It is for that reason that the elder dare not neglect pastoring and teaching in particular. The fifth strand is an indispensable condition of effectiveness in the first four.

We shall be looking in detail at the first four components of the task. But as a preliminary it is necessary to comment on the task of prayer, and on the general responsibility which the elders have to give leadership to the flock.

Prayer

Stress on the importance of prayer is a commonplace among Evangelicals, and the Brethren in particular. Yet while individual Christians and the congregation are exhorted to pray as the pre-condition of blessing, elders do often seem to conduct their activities as though they were purely secular in character, and their meetings as though they were any other business occasion.

There is no reason why elders should not conduct their affairs in a thoroughly orderly way. But a consistent feature of scripture is the need for encounter with God as a condition of effective ministry. We need only consider the cases of Moses, Joshua, Elijah, Isaiah, Jeremiah, Ezekiel and virtually every other figure of note in the leadership of God's people in the Old Testament. In the New, Paul's ministry from the Damascus Road and the Arabian experience onwards was punctuated by direct encounter with God in vision and prophecy, and his teaching as recorded in the epistles was manifestly underpinned by prayer (see *Romans 1:8–11; 1 Corinthians 1:4; Ephesians 1:16–23; Philippians 1:3–11; Colossians 1:3–4, 9–12; 1 Thessalonians 1:2–3;* etc.). In this, Paul was doing no more than to follow the example of Christ, whose ministry was initiated, like that of the Old Testament prophet-leaders, in deep spiritual experience and who, as Luke tells us, resorted to prayer at each crucial moment and decision of his ministry.

The prayer of the elder has both individual and corporate aspects. The need for individual study and prayer, particularly pastoral prayer for members of the flock and for the growth and progress of the congregation as a whole, should scarcely need to be emphasized. Yet it would be a salutary thing for each elder to set down at regular intervals the time spent in the last month in personal Bible study and prayer, preparation for teaching, pastoral work, daily work, leisure, and television-watching respectively.

Similarly, it would be worth the eldership's noting the time spent in the same period in meetings, and the balance between prayer and the transaction of business at them. The role of collective prayer and fasting in selection for Christian service has been noted earlier and the New Testament is insistent on the importance of waiting upon God as the prelude to and environment of Christian service (see, e.g., *Luke 24:49, 53; Acts 1:14; 2:1, 47; 4:24, 31, 33; and 6:2, 4, 7,*—'It is not right that we should give up the word of God to serve tables . . . we will devote ourselves to prayer and to the ministry of the word . . . And the word of God increased; and the number of the disciples multiplied greatly . . .'). It is noticeable that while many Brethren elderships seem content with one meeting a month, often devoted to mechanical arrangements, churches which are showing signs of growth are often characterized by more frequent meetings of elders, some of which are devoted to pastoral matters and prayer—the time sometimes being created sacrificially, *e.g.,* by meetings on Saturdays or early on weekdays.

Leadership

The practicalities of encouraging and enabling the ministry of the whole body will be considered separately. But some general comment is appropriate here on the need for the elders as a body and as individuals to give leadership to the life and ministry of the congregation as a whole. That there is such a need is sometimes questioned on the ground that 'leadership' and 'leading' are not terms commonly found in the New Testament. This view is over-simple. The term is not absent—see, for example, *Luke 2:26* and *Romans 12:8.* And in any case the view does not do justice to the prominence given in scripture to the biographies of great spiritual leaders as the instruments through whom God directed his people on the one hand, nor on the other to the baneful influence of false prophets, wicked kings, and negligent, worldly priests on the experience of the Old Testament people of God. Quite simply, the importance of effective spiritual leadership for the people of God is underscored throughout scripture, and it misses the point in an astonishing way to argue that the terms 'leader' and 'leadership' scarcely appear in the New Testament.

To be sure, there is a difference of emphasis between the Old and New Testaments in that, as prophesied, the lone heroes of

faith in the Old give place in the New to a wider dissemination of
spiritual gift and power, and hence group as distinct from
individual leadership comes into greater relief (though group
leadership was not absent in the Old—cf. the elders called by
Moses to judge Israel, the case of Daniel and his colleagues, and
the team leadership displayed by Haggai, Zechariah, Zerubbabel
and Jeshua as recorded in *Ezra 5:1–2*). Even so, Peter and the
Twelve were looked to for leadership by the early church; Paul and
his colleagues were leaders in missionary enterprise; and at the
Council of Jerusalem the whole church looked to the apostles and
elders to take the lead in dealing with a question of great strategic
importance (see *Acts 15*, especially *4–6, 22*—from our vantage
point, we can easily underestimate the vital significance of the
subject matter of that meeting for the future direction and growth
of the church).

A few years ago, I heard a presentation on managing organisations
which emphasised the importance of a wide range of characteristics
and concerns that leaders of organisations need to possess or
attend to. I was so struck by the relevance to group leadership of
local churches that I noted them down: flexibility; vision; planning;
leadership; motivation; guiding; directing; educating; training;
communication; delegating—not abdicating; monitoring; and decisiveness. Above all, it was said, the main criticism that staff
generally had of their superiors was of their lack of decisiveness—
how often one has heard congregations criticising their leaders for
exactly this fault.

The following chapters touch in different ways on many of these
issues. But in the church leaders require a special characteristic
only touched on in part in the list just given.

Hosea remarked, 'By a prophet the LORD brought Israel up from
Egypt and by a prophet he was preserved.' (*Hosea 12:13*). Moses
and Aaron were the instruments by which God gave Israel the
vision and means to be lifted from the inertia of bondage and
moved out to the land of promise. In the church, prophetic gift and
vision are spread more widely than among the elders. But it is to be
expected that much of that gift will lie with them, and even when
they are not the instrument of vision, it is they who have the
authority in the congregation to determine whether or not it shall
be recognized and responded to. Unequivocally, it is the duty of
the shepherd to lead the flock (*John 10:3–5*). That teaching was
delivered in the context of Jesus's criticism of the blindness of the
Pharisees (*John 9:39–40*) whom elsewhere he condemned as blind
guides of the people (*Matthew 15:14*).

We can speculate about the reasons for antipathy in some parts of the church to the notion of leadership, but there is many an oversight which needs to give hard thought to how it is to fulfil its obligation of giving positive prophetic leadership to the flock.

---

1. 'As a child' is the implication in *Mark 9:36–37*.

4

PASTOR

The importance of pastoring

In the course of church history there have been varying perceptions of the main task of those taking spiritual responsibility in the local church. In the medieval church, the priest's main function would have been considered to be the performance of the central cultic act, the saying or singing of mass on behalf of the people and those departed. The Reformation brought a decisive shift, at least in Calvinist congregations, so that the minister's main task came to be seen to be the preaching of the word, and the layout of church buildings was adapted rigorously to reflect that emphasis. Despite the title of 'pastor', many nonconformist groups in the Anglo-Saxon world continue to see the minister's function as principally that of preaching, and the academic policy and curricula of many theological and Bible colleges still regrettably reflect that.

Such a heavy emphasis seems to lead to a distortion of the five-fold responsibility of the elder which was proposed in the preceding chapter. But before jumping to criticize other non-conformists, we should note the unique distortion to be seen in the Brethren tradition of oversight. If we set aside the propensity to concentrate on the day-to-day minutiae, we should have to acknowledge that the Brethren distortion has been to emphasize the task of discipline to the exclusion of the others. The elders' function has been seen to be the correction and elimination of supposed doctrinal error (usually judged against a distinctive system of dispensational interpretation, or against certain touch-stones, e.g., principles of gathering or prophetic interpretation);

and the maintenance of certain externals of piety (e.g., attendance at the 'morning meeting').

The exercise of doctrinal and pastoral discipline *are* among the obligations of elders. But there would be widespread assent to the proposition that, while attending sometimes with excessive zeal to these matters, Brethren oversights have in general left undone the task of pastoral care. It is the cry of the people that, even more than failure to feed the flock from the word, pastoral care has been superficial, dilatory, or simply neglected. For their part, elders often have to admit that they have to deal with cases as matters of discipline, when earlier and sensitive pastoral action might well have averted any need for discipline. The prophetic strictures against the shepherds of Israel for neglect of the fundamental task of pastoral care need to be taken seriously in our generation. Whatever our doctrinal correctness, if this task is neglected, it will not be surprising that the sheep are scattered and so many congregations find themselves on the verge of extinction.

What is pastoring?

It is a bold man who seeks to encapsulate the nature, requirements and mechanisms of pastoring in a few hundred words. Courses of ministerial training devote many classroom hours to it, and there are many useful textbooks available—the tragedy is that there is in the Brethren an inclination to hold that Christian service can be undertaken by direct divine light without the need to develop the gift which God has given, or to reflect on the nature of the elder's responsibilities.

The essence of the pastoral task can be understood in the metaphors of the shepherd and shepherding. Peter exhorts elders, 'Tend the flock of God that is in your charge . . . willingly . . . eagerly . . . being examples to the flock.' (*1 Peter 5:2–3*) In this image, Peter was drawing upon a deep vein of Old Testament metaphor in which the priestly leaders of the old Israel were viewed as shepherds (see especially *Jeremiah 23:1–4* and *Ezekiel 34 passim*). Peter went on to invoke the Chief Shepherd, who had himself taken up the image and applied it to himself (*see Psalm 23* and *Ezekiel 34, 11, 23*), both in respect of the flock at large (*John 10:1–18*) and individually (*Luke 15:2–7*), and who had commissioned Peter to the same task (*John 21:15–17*—'Feed my sheep').

From this, we are to understand that the pastoral care of God's people entails protecting them, feeding them, healing them, rescuing them, restoring them, and carrying them spiritually, the whole being done with loving care and gentleness, even when exercising the legitimate authority inherent in the elders' right to rule the flock. The task can be grasped succinctly from scripture as the precise opposite of Ezekiel's devastating condemnation of the spiritual leaders of his day (and which can apply to today's congregational leaders too): 'Should not shepherds feed the sheep? You eat the fat, you clothe yourselves with the wool, you slaughter the fatlings, but you do not feed the sheep. The weak you have not strengthened, the sick you have not healed, the crippled you have not bound up, the strayed you have not brought back, the lost you have not sought, and with force and harshness you have ruled them. So they were scattered, because there was no shepherd; . . .' (*Ezekiel 34:2–5*).

Both in its objects and methods, the pastoral task is distinct from that of psychotherapeutic counselling. This is not to argue that counselling does not have a contribution to make to the resolution of some pastoral difficulties: some Christians do suffer from mental and emotional conditions which require specialist care, and pastoral training ought to be sufficient to ensure that the symptoms are recognised at least in a rudimentary way. Nor is it to argue that counselling skills do not have a part to play in effective pastoring. The pastor must listen carefully, and seek insight into the spiritual, emotional and psychological functioning of the person being pastored. Like the counsellor, the pastor cannot do other than to try to bring the pastored to self-understanding and help them to make freer choices about their own life. The Christian pastor needs too to be sensitive to the effects of past, long-forgotten, experiences on people's responses to current situations. Counselling draws on disciplines which have made considerable progress in the last 150 years in understanding the way in which people function—how body, mind and emotion interact. This knowledge should not simply be dismissed as being irrelevant or worse—as fallen creatures, we all have less emotional and psychological control over ourselves than some Christian teaching and advice assumes.

But the Christian pastor claims the right to go beyond at least those counsellors who work within a liberal humanistic framework in which objectives and solutions are largely the client's business, worked out within the framework of his or her own value system. The counsellor's (from one point of view limited) function is to listen, to seek to clarify, and to help the client to work through his difficulties in so far as he is able, in order to permit him to continue to function with reasonable effectiveness as a person. In that sense, the objective is earth-bound. But the Christian claim is that (quite apart from psychological and emotional conditions) temptation, sin and its consequences remain to some extent pervasive in every Christian's life. The Christian pastor is therefore charged to give positive help under the guidance of the Holy Spirit with the objectives of comforting and strengthening those under pressure from the circumstances of life (including the Satanic buffeting to which we are all prey); and of bringing repentance, and amendment and improvement of life, to those whose problem lies within themselves (circumstance and inner life are often reciprocally linked, of course). In short, the pastor's task is in the best sense spiritual strengthening and direction. Those who seek the pastor only to indulge in a species of personal exhibitionism without any real desire to make the changes required to meet their spiritual needs are likely to find Christian pastoring irksome.

The humanist counsellor usually works within a framework of relative truth on the one hand and relative morality on the other. By contrast, the Christian pastor employs the twin instruments of instruction, and correction and reproof (see *2 Timothy 3:16–17*) within the framework of the absolute truth and morality of scripture. In these respects, the pastor must grasp that the task is indissolubly linked with the tasks of preaching the word (a point on which more will be said in the next chapter) and of pastoral discipline. That this is so may be seen in Jesus's dealings with, for example, the woman at the well (*John 4:7–26*), his constant work with his disciples, and in his resurrection appearances, e.g., to the two on the road to Emmaus (*Luke 24:13–35*), to Thomas (*John 20:24–29*), and to Peter (*John 21:15–19*). Similarly, pastoral methods can readily be seen throughout the epistles, which are all pastoral in character, especially *1 & 2 Corinthians*.

The requirements of the pastor

To define the pastor's task and method so positively would be presumptuous, but for scripture. It is an onerous responsibility and, if undertaken in the flesh, is open to serious abuse, as can be seen from contemporary and earlier church history. The pastor needs to have a close personal walk with God and *spiritual* rather than natural gifts, e.g., those of the pastor, of discernment and of knowledge—there will be times when, like Peter confronted with

Ananias and Sapphira (*Acts 5:1–11*), perception of personal needs and problems will have to be supernatural.

The pastor will also need the pastor's heart: that loving concern and anguish for individual Christians and the congregation which Paul displayed when he admonished the Ephesian church with tears (*Acts 20:31*) and when he wrote to the Corinthians 'out of much affliction and anguish of heart and with many tears, not to cause you pain but to let you know of the abundant love that I have for you'. (*2 Corinthians 2:4*) Like Moses, he is charged, 'Carry them in your bosom, as a nurse carries the sucking child' (*Numbers 11:12*).

The pastor also needs the ability to listen carefully and perceptively rather than to do all the talking (the real problem may not be the one which has been raised), and to command confidence and to encourage others to unburden themselves. To that end, the pastor will need to devote time to the task, and to be patient with the limitations and foibles even of the best. And the pastor will need above all the talent to teach, often unobtrusively and always sensitively, in pastoral conversation, from a position which is alongside the pastored, not above him or her.

Formal and informal pastoring

Except in disciplinary matters, the pastoral tradition of the Brethren is informal in character. The assumption is that pastoral work is to be done in the ordinary course of fellowship in the church. It is a valuable tradition: much pastoral work *must* be done in that way, for even the best ordered and most diligent eldership will not find it possible to arrange for each of their number to hold more than a handful of pastoral interviews in the course of a year. At all times, whether in meeting members individually or socially or at church meetings, elders should seek to be open and available to the flock (in particular, the temptation to transact business between elders should be resisted as far as possible); they should take an interest in the spiritual and practical concerns of church members; and they should be alert for the signs of need (they should be on the lookout, for example, for the unusually silent, or those who seem troubled). In the process, valuable opportunities for pastoral conversation may arise, though the elder should remember that the deeper and more sensitive matters should not be discussed with a third party listening in.

The *advantage* of such continuous and 'informal' pastoring is that it profits from relations of confidence built up in the give-and-take of ordinary fellowship. People are more likely to be relaxed and unable to strike poses as they might in a formal situation. The *disadvantages* are however that it is easy to slip from informal pastoring to doing none at all, i.e., it is simply neglected, and hard questions are ducked. There are many matters, particularly serious ones and those which may turn into disciplinary cases, which are better dealt with formally because it is then easier to get to the nub of the matter.

Apart from these considerations, some require definite visitation: the elderly, the shut-in, the sick and the bereaved. Formal arrangements are needed, too, for those contemplating marriage— it is an unhealthy tradition in Brethrenism that engagement and marriage are regarded as purely private matters with the arrangements at the disposition of the couple and the family, rather than of legitimate pastoral concern to the elders and the congregation.

It would also be a desirable development in many churches for the elders to adopt the practice of finding out the addresses of those visiting the church for the first time and, if they live in the locality, to arrange to call on them at an early date. In some instances there would be evangelistic opportunities. If the person is already a Christian but without definite church connexion, the care and interest signified by a visit from an elder might well cement the initial relationship with the fellowship.

The great advantage of formal arrangements for visitation, *as a reinforcement to informal pastoring*, is that it should ensure that no one is neglected, as is all too easy in the informal system. Secondly, formal arrangements should help the elders to keep their pastoral obligations and objectives firmly in view. And beyond personal and spiritual needs, they enable the elders to consult church members in a systematic way about matters of common interest in the fellowship, and to discuss the personal contribution of the individual to its life.

Organization for pastoring

Where pastoral work is being done by a plural eldership, some kind of organization and co-ordination is needed if, on the one hand, some needs are not to be neglected and, on the other, confusing duplication and triplication of activity is to be avoided.

The precise arrangements will have to be adjusted to the needs and circumstances of the particular fellowship. The following are only some suggestions which may be useful, at least in part.

Neglect can be avoided if the eldership make it a practice to review the needs of each member of the fellowship at regular intervals, for example, by systematic consideration of the list of members. A further step is to allocate to each elder, monthly, an individual whom they are to visit. (Incidentally, there is no reason why most pastoral visitation may not be done singly—if the tradition of pairs is followed, the burden of the task will be doubled.) An alternative is to divide the congregation between the elders by area so that the resulting group form a sub-flock which is the special responsibility of one or two elders who are charged to visit formally each individual in the group, say, at least once a year. Where the fellowship meets in home or area groups for Bible study, prayer and fellowship, those groups can form natural pastoral units for the elder or elders in each group and others with pastoral gift can easily be drawn into the work.

Whatever the arrangement, it is desirable to have some form of reporting back to the eldership so that all are aware of the more important matters and so that all the elders are kept up to the mark in the task. The elders may also find it helpful to charge one suitably-gifted elder with the task of co-ordination of the elders' pastoral work. Such an individual can act as a point of contact for the church members when emergency action is needed. That person can draw into pastoral work appropriate people with pastoral gift outside the eldership, particularly women. Above all the co-ordinator can see to it that whatever pastoral arrangements have been adopted are being properly executed by the elders. Frequently, this will be a natural task for a full-time elder if that person has the appropriate gifts.

In any case, it is to be expected that a considerable portion of time each month will be spent by the elders in considering pastoral needs together and in praying about them. Whoever prepares the agenda for such meetings should try to help by identifying particular individuals who may need to be considered. All pastoral work needs to be prepared and reinforced in prayer on the part of the elder personally and of the eldership as a body. It should be undertaken equally systematically, with the list of members in hand.

The prize of pastoring

If elderships give greater thought to the practice of pastoring and to arrangements to achieve a major improvement of pastoral care in their churches, there is a very great prize to be grasped. This is nothing less than the consolidation of their flocks as effective units for spiritual growth and outreach—the very opposite of the scattering which will flow from its neglect.

5

TEACHER

The need for settled teaching

It was noted at the beginning of the previous chapter that certain nonconformist groups have tended to define the task of the congregational leader mainly as that of teaching the flock. In arguing that that task can be emphasized to the point of distorting the biblical pattern, we should not, however, lose our balance and conclude that the elder needs no more than a warm personality and gifts of counselling and wisdom. We should not suggest that the teaching gift is optional.

For there is a paradox to be seen in the recent religious culture of the Brethren. On the one hand, scripture is rightly regarded as the sole determinant of Christian faith and practice (which is not to argue that the principle is always applied in practice). Historically, the Brethren are virtually unique among the mature denominations in doing without formal creeds, confessions, statements of faith, articles of association, and canon law. The ground for this is that scripture itself is the statement of faith, and efforts to reduce the most important teachings of scripture to a set of theses which are *ipso facto* additional to scripture is bound to be fraught with doctrinal danger (which is not to argue that the characteristic systems of Brethren interpretation and principles, passed on from generation to generation mainly by word of mouth, have not constituted as binding a set of statements which are additional to scripture).

In the first fifty years of this century this regard for scripture enabled the Brethren in many places to perform a great service to Anglo-Saxon protestantism in being one of the main vehicles for the preservation of evangelical faith. But the paradox lies in the fact that increasingly the principle of *sola scriptura* has been left to operate in the private study of the individual: the arrangements for teaching in the congregations have not normally been conducive to coherent teaching of the body of faith as revealed in scripture.

First, there has been the emphasis, derived from a theologically charismatic perception of the nature of ministry, that the word is to be preached without careful preparation, by this or that individual as led at the particular moment under the influence of the Spirit. This emphasis has militated against systematic teaching and has been abused wherever it has been supposed that teaching can be effective without spiritual and mental exercise on the part of the teacher.

Secondly, there is the habit—now waning in many congregations —that formal teaching should normally be undertaken by individuals from outside the particular congregation, so that the 'corresponding brother' considered himself highly competent if he succeeded in attracting 104 different speakers in the year to the 'Gospel Service' and the mid-week teaching meeting.

This is a caricature. Nor is it meant to imply that no place should be given to prophetic utterance, whether itinerant or resident, to itinerant evangelists and church-planters, or to itinerant teachers who exercise a powerful inter-congregational ministry. (The comparative lack of people who exercise an influence similar to that of, say, John Stott, Roger Forster, Michael Green and Gerald Coates in their respective circles, is symptomatic of the current weakness of the Brethren movement.) But, in my judgement, there remains a prime need for Brethren congregations to discover or recover an understanding of the importance of a congregational teaching ministry which lies primarily in the hands of those responsible to God for the faithfulness of their congregations to, *inter alia*, the faith once delivered, i.e., the elders.

Teaching: a fundamental and essential task

A precondition of such a discovery or recovery is an understanding, on the part of the elders and the congregation alike, of the importance of teaching and preaching in creating and building Christian faith and life. Of its very nature, Christianity is a revealed religion. The vehicle of revelation, and the means of its preservation, is the word—in the Old Testament, the law (the ten words) and the former and the latter prophets; in the New, the witness of the apostles and, above all, of the Living Word. He was himself a rabbi (teacher). A principal component of his ministry was teaching (see, e.g., *Matthew 5:28; 10:35;* and *11:7*) and it is that component which endures for us in the gospels more than his ministry of healing and other miracles. It is not therefore accidental that one of the main effects, both of his own coming and that of the Holy Spirit, was a new release of the prophetic word (cf., *Luke 1 & 2 passim;* and *Acts 2:17–18*) and the launching of the church on a ministry of teaching and preaching—'Go therefore and make *disciples . . . teaching* them to observe all that I have commanded you; . . .' (*Matthew 28:19–20;* cf. also *Matthew 10:7, 14, 24–25*). One of the main purposes in the giving of the Holy Spirit was to equip the church both with the truth and the ability to communicate it (*John 16:13*). 'How,' wrote Paul, 'are they to believe in him of whom they have never heard? And how are they to hear without a preacher? . . . So faith comes from what is heard, and what is heard comes by the preaching of Christ' (*Romans 10:14, 17*). Both the gospels and the epistles stand as a monument to the fundamental importance of teaching the truth in the building of the kingdom of God.

If this is the emphasis of scripture, it is not surprising that the one skill, as distinct from quality, which Paul is emphatic should be possessed by the elder is that of apt teaching (*1 Timothy 3:2*). The elder should be able to 'hold firm to the sure word as taught' and 'to give instruction in sound doctrine and also to confute those who contradict it' (*Titus 1:9*). It also explains why Paul considered Timothy's teaching gifts so important (*1 Timothy 4:13–16*) and why he considered those who laboured in preaching and teaching worthy of double honour (*1 Timothy 5:17*).

The emphasis requires elders to give hard thought to the nature of an effective teaching ministry, to how it is to be made lively and interesting, and to how a body of elders are to succeed individually and collectively in ensuring that their congregation is receiving teaching of the required nature. If they do not do so, they will be guilty of one of the worst things in which elders can fail—leaving the flock unfed.

The three-fold nature of teaching

The boredom and impatience of many ordinary church-members with the teaching which they receive can often be traced to the shortcomings of those who teach, to the imperfect understanding of the teachers of their responsibilities, to their penchant for making dull what should be lively, exciting and vibrant, and even to their laziness so much as to learn to use an overhead projector effectively.

It is a common error today to identify Christian teaching with secular education within the humanist framework of thought. Despite the influence of romanticism and existentialism, this tends to give primacy to the mind, to the exclusion of heart, will and imagination. Further, it confines discourse to phenomena which can be fitted within a natural framework, so that the supernatural is excluded by presupposition. In consequence, teaching is about the communication of fact and theories to be apprehended intellectually, without necessary spiritual, emotional or practical effects.

Unhappily, this trend has taken deep root in Brethren spirituality (and some other Evangelical quarters) in the last two generations, so that it has become essentially cerebral in nature, even among those whose education has been comparatively limited. Nowhere has this trend had more effect than in worship and teaching, with the result that many in our congregations find both processes boring and unrewarding. There is a danger that spirituality will sink into no more than a dead orthodoxy—'you have a name of being alive, and you are dead' (*Revelation 3:1*). In consequence, it is no wonder that many churches make so little impact especially with young people.

In the case of teaching, there is a need to recover its three-fold nature:
(1)   that its aim is coherent knowledge of the truth;
(2)   that its proper context is a perception of the pastoral needs of the congregation; and
(3)   that its power lies in prophetic immediacy.

Coherent instruction

It is important that the baby be not thrown out with the bath water: disillusion with dead orthodoxy should not lead us to despise orthodoxy (provided that its tenets are indeed justified on grounds of scripture!). We have already noted that the Master's command was to teach *all* that he commanded (*Matthew 28:19*) and Paul's clear implication was that the elders of Ephesus should, like him, not shrink from declaring to the church 'the whole counsel of God' (*Acts 20:27*). Scripture as a whole comprises a body of truth which needs to be taught systematically to the church in a manner which is well adjusted to the various different levels of knowledge which have been attained by the various members of the congregation.

That body of truth is the firm foundation for the life and practice of the individual Christian and of the congregation. Without it, the edifice will always be in danger of crumbling (*Matthew 7:24–27*) and there will be a risk of fundamental error which will result in the scattering of the flock (*Acts 20:29–32*).

The pastoral context

The common method of organizing teaching in the Brethren in the past has often frustrated any hope of achieving a full-orbed appreciation of the truth. But, on its own, coherent instruction is not enough. Both the method of organizing, and secular concepts of the nature of, teaching have also threatened to obscure the realization that if Christian teaching, however balanced and accurate, is to have any real fruit in the congregation, it *must* be pastoral in character. The purpose of teaching is not simply to impart theological information and ideas: it is to feed so as to sustain life and bring about growth. One possible reading of *Ephesians 4:11* draws no sharp distinction between the gifts of pastor and teacher, but would view the words as a reference to a composite gift of pastor-and-teacher. Such a rendering is lent support by Paul's advice to the elders at Ephesus in which he identified the pastoral task of feeding the flock with declaring the whole counsel of God (*Acts 20:27*) and constant admonition (*v.31*); and indeed by the epistles as a whole.

This has two implications. First, there is a need for teaching to grow out of pastoral experience: it is the task of the teacher to know the flock individually and collectively, and to use the perceptions which that gives of the current needs of the flock as a basis for determining the subjects and thrust of teaching. Secondly, it follows that teaching should be a major way in which pastoral needs are met. Knowing the needs, the teachers should be able to teach so that the congregation finds that the instruction speaks to their perceived needs and therefore comforts them, strengthens them to cope with problems and to overcome sin and temptation, and imparts vision and guidance to help in daily life and service.

None of this excludes the work of the Holy Spirit. The gift of itinerants must enable them to perceive pastoral need supernaturally, while resident elders need discernment to identify the unspoken needs of those whom they know well. But where pastoral need is not met, teaching is likely to be regarded as dry and irrelevant, i.e., the flock is not fed.

Prophetic immediacy

It was a serious matter when Israel lacked the prophetic voice (see *1 Samuel 3:1*). The Old Testament is characterized by the proposition that God reveals himself to his people for a variety of purposes by the prophet. That strain continues in the New Testament, arguably in an enhanced way (see *Acts 2:17–18* as already cited; *Romans 12:6; 1 Corinthians 12:10, 28–29; 13:2;* and 14 *passim*). The early church was led not simply by pastor and teachers, but by pastors, teachers and prophets who together contributed to the building up, encouragement, consolation and direction of the congregation. Moreover, by comparing *Acts 11;26–28, 13:1–3* and *15:30–35,* it can be seen that the prophets not only uttered predictions which became the basis of congregational action (*Acts 11:27–30*) and were the vehicle of divine leading of the congregation (*Acts 13:2*); they also 'exhorted the brethren with many words and strengthened them' (*Acts 15:32*). These teaching and pastoral tasks were explicitly linked with prophecy by Paul when he asserted, as a matter of principle, '. . . he who prophesies speaks to men for their upbuilding and encouragement and consolation . . . he who prophesies edifies the church . . . I would rather speak five words with my mind, in order to instruct others . . .' (*1 Corinthians 14:3, 5, 19*).

This is not the place for a detailed examination of the nature of prophecy in scripture.[1] Let it suffice to say that the prophet's task in the Old Testament was frequently to speak a word from God which was of immediate and pressing relevance to the belief, worship and life of the people. In this, the prophets revealed the person and purposes of God (i.e., they taught the people) and they ministered to their pastoral needs. Above all, it was a word revealed directly under the influence of the Spirit of the Living God, and if teaching is to be effective in our day it continues to be essential for it to be done by people who are gripped by the Holy Spirit and know what he wishes to say to the church.

From this we can see that the gifts of the teacher, the pastor and the prophet are not so much self-contained but rather comprise a field within which the elders as a body must seek to operate. It is true that the gifts of one may be centred towards teaching, of another more towards pastoring, and of a third more towards prophecy. But the links between the gifts seem so strong in the New Testament that one will rarely be found without some measure of the other two. The tragedy is that teaching so often lacks the pastoral purpose which will establish its relevance to the hearers and the prophetic immediacy which will stir them up to take action on what they hear.

Achieving a pastoral and prophetic teaching ministry

Under the traditional arrangements of Lutheran (including Anglican) and Reformed churches, there is no great practical obstacle to achieving coherent teaching which is relevant to pastoral needs. Coherence is achievable because the task of teaching falls to a single mind. Pastoral relevance is secured because the task of teaching falls to the man (usually still) responsible for the bulk of the pastoral work. Whether it is prophetic depends very much on the man. The question for those in the Brethren tradition (and for others developing team leadership of the local church) is how a plural eldership with gifts differing in character and degree is to achieve the purposes suggested in this chapter.

We should not underestimate the ability of the sovereign Spirit to blend the gifts of *Ephesians 4:11* to build a mature congregation so that 'joined and knit together by every joint with which it is supplied, when each part is working properly, [it] makes bodily growth and upbuilds itself in love' (*Ephesians 4:13, 16*). We should not however exclude the possibility that the elders as a body are expected to make a conscious contribution to this process by seeing themselves as responsible for the teaching of the church (if it seems desirable to divert the task to others they should ask themselves whether they should be continuing in eldership) and by taking steps to provide, by means of their own and other gifts in the congregation, a coherent teaching ministry of the kind discussed.

Whether this is done formally or informally is of no great importance in itself. But it will often be desirable for the elders, or at least those upon whom the main burden of teaching falls, to meet regularly for prayer and discussion, with the explicit aims:

(1) of considering the pastoral needs of the congregation, in order to identify the subjects and priorities for teaching in the immediate future;

(2) of ensuring that in the longer run there is a due balance given to study of the various parts of scripture;

(3) of planning how the various subjects and passages shall be dealt with and deciding who shall teach, taking into account the various gifts and qualities of the main teachers in the congregation; and of planning the contribution to be sought from those from outside the congregation;

(4)   of ensuring that so far as possible each teacher understands
thoroughly what it is under God that the body of teachers are
seeking to achieve in any particular programme of teaching; and
(5)   of adjusting the programme and arrangements for teaching to
the various levels of understanding in the congregation—it is a
fault of Brethren churches, as of many other evangelical congregations, to assume that once a person has been converted and
baptized they should be able to be taught alongside those who
have been many years on the path of faith.

Greater attention to subject matter and to coherence can be
expected to show early benefits in the congregation. The elders
will soon find that they are able to use the teaching given to
provide the church with a lead in directions which they perceive to
be necessary, e.g., in seeking to deepen its understanding of
worship, or in stirring it up to greater evangelistic effort. For teaching is a primary instrument of leadership.

In making more structured arrangements, however, it would not
be wise to tie everything down too much. The elders as well as the
congregation may need the opportunity to be able to respond to
God's message for the moment, which may not have been foreseen
in advance. But this implies not so much making no plans, as
allowing the flexibility for them to be changed, even at short
notice, if that seems the right thing to do. The good leader is one
who knows when it is right to adjust to present requirements
as well as when it is right to stick doggedly to the original purpose
whatever the distractions.

---

1.   I take it for granted that the New Testament does not assume that the gift of
the prophet will die with the completion of the canon of scripture. On the gift of
prophecy, see *inter alia* Wayne Grudem, *The Gift of Prophecy in the New Testament and
today*, Eastbourne: Kingsway Publications, 1988; and David E. Aune, *Prophecy in
Early Christianity and the Ancient Mediterranean World*, Grand Rapids, Michigan:
Eerdmans, 1983.

6

RULER

For a generation the concepts of authority and discipline have been unpopular. As usual, Christians have not been slow to assimilate prevailing opinions. It is true that in earlier generations and in particular parts of the Brethren movement there has been a tendency to misuse the authority of the elder and of the congregation. It is also true that more effective teaching and better pastoral care will frequently succeed in avoiding the need for disciplinary action. But despite the indwelling Holy Spirit, Christians remain imperfect in this life and on occasion pastoral discipline will be a sad necessity.

The concept of discipline implies that there is authority (i.e., right and power) to enforce it and exact due penalty. Before considering how discipline should be exercised by the elder, it is worth reflecting on the nature of this authority.

The authority of the elder

Humanly speaking, the origin of the office of elder lies in the Jewish world in which the church was born. Legal power in the religious and civil spheres (insofar as they may be distinguished) was exercised by elders from Hebrew antiquity: Moses appointed officials bearing this designation (*Numbers 11:10–29*)[1] and *Deuteronomy* envisages that in the land of promise judicial authority in each city shall be in the hands of elders. At the national level, the 'elders of the people' continued in some form or another through the period of the Judges and the monarchy into the Exile and beyond. From the New Testament we can see that by the time of Christ, the chief priests, the elders of the people, and the scribes (legal advisers) constituting the Sanhedrin had legal power in doctrine and practice and the authority to apply penalties, subject only to the sanction of the Roman procurator in cases of capital punishment. At the local level, the synagogue, which was a model from which the structures of the early church were drawn, was governed by elders, who had civil as well as religious functions and power to punish by means of scourging and excommunication.

The basic function of the administration of the law in the old Israel was to preserve the covenant holiness of the people. The apostles regarded themselves, and the elders whom they appointed, as possessing similar responsibility towards the new Israel. Thus Paul frequently represents himself as entitled to command obedience from individual Christians (*Philemon 7, 21*) and from the congregation (*2 Corinthians 1:23–2:2; 13:2*); and, even in his absence from the congregation concerned, to impose disciplinary penalty (*1 Corinthians 5:3–5*). Similarly, he regards elders as entitled to exercise authority in the church: those who rule or direct well are to be considered worthy of double honour and the context shows that that rule extended to rebuking those who persist in sin (*1 Timothy 5:17–21*). The implication of one of the elder's qualifications is that he should be capable of managing the church in the same way as the father was expected to manage the extended household of the Graeco-Roman world (*1 Timothy 3:4–5*). If necessary, the elder may admonish and rebuke 'sharply' (*Titus 1:13*; see also *Acts 20:31; 1 Thessalonians 5:12*). In turn, the congregation is enjoined to respect those who have been placed over them in the Lord and to submit themselves to their authority (*1 Thessalonians 5:12; 1 Peter 5:5*; see also *1 Corinthians 16:16*).

This outline contains no surprises to those in the Brethren tradition, though it may bear repetition to a generation with too great a respect for anarchy and to any whose concept of spiritual liberty threatens the principle of due order, of which the elder is expected to be the guardian. But too frequently, for elder and congregation alike, the analysis ends here. Biblically, legitimate authority from God is intended to have the beneficial results of reconciliation, health and ordered harmony, of *shalom* in the sense of the Old Testament. A moment's reflection on the reality of the exercise of authority in the church, not just in Brethren assemblies, suggests however that this is not always the effect. The painful fact is that, on the one hand, legitimate authority is not always respected and, on the other, that elders can and do abuse it. So we need to ask ourselves what are the main *purposes* for which it should be used; what are the proper *penalties* which may be imposed and when; and what are the *checks* and *balances* of substance and process which are intended to protect the congregation and the individual against the abuse of power.

The scope of authority

In the following paragraphs, the main uses of the elder's authority are (to assist exposition and understanding) divided into two groups, though in fact there is no clear distinction between them in principle. First, there are items which are usually uncontroversial and may be gathered under the heading of *regulation*. Secondly, there are more controversial matters of *pastoral discipline*, which are so because they may *in extremis* entail the imposition of penalties.

Regulation

There are three obvious matters which the elders need to regulate as a matter of course in the day-to-day life of the congregation.

First, there is admission to fellowship including initiation in baptism. When Paul went up to Jerusalem after his conversion, he implies that his credentials were examined by Peter and James, the brother of the Lord (*Galatians 1:18–19*): and Luke tells us that Barnabas represented him by giving account of his conversion and his subsequent ministry (*Acts 9:27*). There were special circumstances as Paul was a former persecutor of the church. But elsewhere in Acts there is reference to a request that a local congregation should receive an individual, which implies control of reception, and immediately afterwards we see Paul examining those who in their beliefs were at that time on the fringe of true fellowship in the church (*Acts 18:27; 19:1–7*). The new Israel can be seen to be a gathered community of those who have been sanctified in Christ, i.e., of genuine Christians and, in the apostles' footsteps, the elders are intended to use their authority with the aim of preserving the covenant holiness of the church—though, as elders are fallible, it should be remembered that it can never be wholly achieved.

It is doubtful whether the early church regulated membership in the systematic manner commonly found today, e.g., by maintaining formal lists of membership. But for the practical reasons already discussed in the context of pastoral responsibility, it is desirable to know who is in definite relationship with the congregation. Moreover, in admitting individuals to that relationship, its privileges and obligations can be discussed and it can be made clear that membership implies acceptance of the elders' pastoral authority. It may also be worth keeping two further lists: a register of baptisms, as memory may not be wholly reliable, nor the minutes of elders' meetings complete and readily accessible; and a supplementary list of those who may not have committed themselves to the congregation but who are closely associated with it and no other. The pastoral authority of the elders over the latter individuals may be ambiguous, but in my judgement the elders should regard themselves as having pastoral obligations towards them. (It would be interesting to explore the proposition that to submit oneself to the pastoral authority of the elders of one congregation is to submit oneself to those of a congregation with which one happens to be sharing temporary fellowship.)

These are important practical matters in days in which people see themselves as having increasingly loose associations with specific congregations—days in which, for better or worse, Christians do judge local churches like supermarkets whose products demand loyalty only so long as their quality and packaging is thought to be of high quality. Given these attitudes, the risk that individuals will fall through the pastoral net is very great.

Secondly, under the old and new covenants, marriage is regarded not as a private contract between individuals or families, but as of fundamental importance to the fortunes of the people of God. Divorce is now widespread among those who may subsequently become Christians, and among Christians too. It is wise for the elders to take a close interest in those who intend to marry within the fellowship and therefore under the authority of the elders. They need to evolve guidelines as to who may be married under that authority. There is here a strong pastoral aspect: pastors in most denominations find it desirable to invest much pastoral effort in preparing Christians for marriage and, when Christians take the marriage and family bond so lightly, it would be curious if all pastors were not to take this responsibility seriously. Pastoral care, if necessary leading to regulation, is needed for those whose marriages are in difficulty. And for those who are divorced, a high degree of care may be needed, even if there is no reason for discipline in respect of them. It is not accidental that Paul devotes much space to these matters (*1 Corinthians 7; 2 Corinthians 6:14–7:1*). Moreover, relationships of other kinds may cause others to stumble or they may threaten open scandal for the fellowship; pastoral regulation and discipline may need, for example, to extend on occasion to matters arising from business relationships.

Thirdly, there is the responsibility of regulating worship. This was one of the chief functions of the elders in the synagogue (see *Acts 13:15; Luke 4:16–30*). It is not immediately explicit that elders in the early church had similar responsibilities. But they were certainly to control teaching (see *Titus 2:10–11*). While *1 Corinthians* is addressed to the whole church (the import of this fact for discipline will be considered later), it was not the body but the prophets among them who were to control prophetic utterance in congregational worship (*1 Corinthians 14:29, 32*). There does not seem much room to doubt that responsibility for giving effect to the command, 'all things should be done decently and in order' (*1 Corinthians 14:40*) rests primarily with the elders who are otherwise responsible for regulating the congregation's life.

If they are to discharge this responsibility effectively, they had better give advance thought both to biblically-acceptable forms of contribution, especially in open worship, and to procedures for exercising control *in extremis*. For example, where certain spiritual gifts purport to be exercised, the elders need to know what is a valid prophecy, tongue, or interpretation. And it is hardly possible to convene an elders' meeting in the course of such a contribution to decide whether it is edifying: the elders will probably need to appoint a president for each occasion to apply their guidelines *if necessary*. Normally, of course, control can and should be exercised discreetly *post hoc*.

It is also desirable that the elders should work out together from scripture, and with due regard for the historic practice of the universal church, guidelines to assist them in regulating baptism, admission to fellowship (including of those who are known to have fallen into grave sin), marriage and divorce. The term 'guideline' is used advisedly, not so much because of the well-known problems of applying rules to cases, but because no formulation which is of its nature distinct from scripture should be regarded as final; it must be subject to the possibility of amendment as in time more light breaks forth from holy scripture.

Pastoral discipline

Reference to the control of teaching and to divorce leads conveniently to more controversial matters. For it is when authority is applied in questions of doctrine and personal morality that its disciplinary implications become most obvious.

The legitimacy and desirability of proper discipline in these matters is beyond doubt. The New Testament insists on the elders' obligation to guard the church in its doctrine (*Acts 20:27–32* and *Titus 1:9–16*). Paul recognized the right of those in authority to examine him in respect of the truth of his teaching (*Galatians 2:2*) and he enjoined Titus to exhort and rebuke those guilty of unsound teaching and unholy life alike 'with all authority.' 'Let no one disregard you' (*Titus 2:15*). And the Corinthians were given precise instructions as to the action which they were to take against those guilty of gross and persistent sin such as sexual immorality, idolatry, verbal abuse, drunkenness or theft (*1 Corinthians 6*).

The reality of this authority can be measured by the *penalties* which were prescribed. Under the old Covenant, the holiness of God's people was to be preserved from doctrinal error (blasphemy) and gross sin by death. In respect of blasphemy and adultery, Jesus' contemporaries appeared sometimes to contemplate capital punishment (see *John 8:1–11, 59*) while, as already noted, in the synagogue scourging and excommunication were the sanctions. The gospel however brought a decisive shift in the church, so that the ultimate sanctions are confined to silencing the false teacher (*Titus 1:11*) and, if necessary, excommunicating both him and the gross sinner who does not repent (see *1 Corinthians 5:3, 9–13; Titus 3:9–11; 2 John 9–11*). Any further sanction is seen as lying in the hands of God, sometimes through the agency of Satan and sometimes in sickness and death, though the apostles on occasion appear to have claimed a somewhat positive role in the process (if this is doubted, refer to *Acts 5:5, 10; 1 Corinthians 5:5; 1 Corinthians 16:22; Galatians 1:9; 1 Timothy 1:20; Revelation 2:22–23*. See also *Romans 12:19–21* and *1 Corinthians 11:30*).

Checks and balances

Attenuated though they are compared with those of the old covenant, silence and banning from fellowship are still what Lord Denning would have called 'very big sticks indeed' in the hands of power. Authority can easily be abused and scripture provides checks and balances both of substance and process.

As to substance, let the comparatively limited ambit of discipline be noted. As Paul reminded Timothy with himself as the example (*1 Timothy 1:12–16*), elders are no more than saved sinners who have received the mercy of God. So the epistles are clear that excommunication is reserved for flagrant and persistent sin which scandalizes (i.e., causes to stumble) both congregation and world. Every spiritual ruler must guard against using authority in the manner of the scribe and Pharisee—evangelicals are more open to this danger than others. For its part, the charge of false teaching relates not to matters upon which sound and reputable teachers are themselves divided, but to matters of great doctrinal moment, to the foundational truths of the church. In the New Testament, the issues are the nature of the Godhead, the person of Christ, and the ground of salvation. The myths, endless genealogies, dissensions and quarrels over the law, to which Paul refers in *1 & 2 Timothy* and *Titus*, were significant in this context because their contenders were seeking to substitute knowledge of such arcane matters for the apostolic ground of salvation. Elders who seek to make inessential matters the touchstone of fellowship are putting themselves in the position of such teachers, not of their apostolic judges.

It should go without saying that the elders must in their exercise of authority themselves be subject to the rule of scripture. In instructing Timothy, Paul is explicit that his instructions are to be regarded as rules which are to be kept (*1 Timothy* 5:21). Elders and their congregations need to measure the elders' administration against both scripture and the guidelines which they may have set for themselves on any particular matter. It follows that the elders will need to explain their decisions and actions to the congregation.

Further, elders must always regard discipline as a last resort, in the same way as divine judgement is revealed in scripture as a last resort. The elders' first recourse when faced even with serious error or sin is to be pastoral: to reason with the individual concerned 'out of much affliction and anguish of heart and with many tears, not to cause you pain but to let you know the abundant love that I have for you' (*2 Corinthians* 2:4; see also *Acts* 20:31). The object is by loving and gentle instruction to encourage repentance as a basis for forgiveness and restitution (*2 Corinthians* 2:5–11; and *2 Timothy* 2:23–26).[2] At the very least, due warning is prescribed (*2 Corinthians* 13:2; *Titus* 3:10).

Due and fair process before discipline is administered is the inflexible requirement of scripture. Rule is to be applied 'without favour, doing nothing from partiality.' (*1 Timothy* 5:21). Any charge against a believer, whether an elder (*1 Timothy* 5:19) or otherwise (*2 Corinthians* 13:2), must be sustained by the evidence of two or three direct witnesses. The accused must also be confronted properly with the charge and given the opportunity to account for himself or herself (*Matthew 18:15–17*).

Further, discipline is not to be administered by any elder on their own. In the passage just cited, the Lord required that a charge should be heard by one or two others and not just the accuser. In *1 Corinthians 14*, Paul requires that the prophet shall be tested by the prophets in the plural. Even further, the Lord proposed that discipline should be executed ultimately by the whole congregation ('If he refuses to listen to them, tell it to the church; and if he refuses to listen even to the church, let him be to you as a Gentile and a tax collector.'—*Matthew 18:17*). This was consistent with the principle of the old covenant that execution should be carried out by judge and people alike (and not by a mercenary executioner) (cf. *John 8, loc. cit.* and *Acts 7:58–59* and *8:1*). The epistles prescribe similarly that the ban from fellowship should be imposed by the congregation, not simply by the elders (see e.g., *1 Corinthians 5:5* and *2 Corinthians 2:6*). It follows that the elders' exercise of discipline must be public, not private, and that the elders must be prepared to be questioned about it by the congregation.

The genius of divine revelation here is that in putting ultimate responsibility with the body of a whole, the risk of arbitrary exercise of power by an individual or by the elders collectively is to some extent contained. The elders' rule is subject to the confirmation of the congregation and in that sense the elders must recognise that while they are ultimately accountable to God, they are answerable temporally to the congregation too. This is a principle which deserves careful thought.

The proper exercise of authority can easily lapse into authoritarianism. Little has been said about it in this chapter, but in religous groups which combine spiritual intensity and the voluntary loyalty of the adherents, the possibility of unjustified interference of the leader in the minutiae of the lives of the members is real. In the past some Brethren congregations have not been exempt from it. The checks and balances which have been described are vitally important in that context.

---

1. It seems reasonable to suppose that the function will have been partly judicial, though the officials appointed for that purpose on Jethro's advice (*Exodus 18:13–27*) are not described as elders.
2. It is interesting that Peter's question leading to the Lord's teaching on the scope of forgiveness follows immediately the Lord's teaching on how to handle sin in the congregation (*Matthew 18:15–35*).

7

LEADER

This chapter returns to an issue of great importance. In discussing the tasks of the elder, the need for congregational leadership was stressed as a matter of principle. The purpose of this chapter is to consider the task of leadership in more detail because of its intrinsic importance in facilitating the spiritual and numerical growth of the congregation and because of the danger that elders will neglect its importance with the result that their congregations will suffer through loss of morale and purpose. For elders are often well aware that they must pastor, teach and (when necessary) discipline; and they make conscientious attempts to carry out these tasks. But they can be insufficiently aware that leadership is one of the prime purposes for which these tasks are undertaken, with the result that their oversight has something of a caretaking character. While conscientious work is done, neither they nor the congregation are presented with any serious challenge to growth, and stagnation or decline can be the result.

The special character of Christian leadership

It can be argued that at the extremes there are two views of leadership to be found in evangelical congregations. The first identifies the leader's task as himself to undertake the bulk of the spiritual and other distinctively Christian work within the congregation; in this understanding, the members of the congregation are little more than attenders and consumers of the spiritual product of those recognized as congregational leaders. At the other extreme—and in reaction to the first—is the characteristic Brethren understanding: not only are the various tasks of ministry and service widely devolved upon members of the congregation, but so, too, is leadership.

In their different ways, both these understandings are a negation of the concept of leadership. The latter denies the need for it and can be characterized as a form of anarchy. In the former, since there is little or no activity on the part of the congregation, there is no requirement for the relationship which constitutes leadership.

Resistance in Brethren circles to the idea that certain individuals in a congregation should take the lead in congregational life by reason of gift and office has both practical and theoretical sources. Sometimes resistance can be attributed to plain envy, as in any other type of group. In Christian groups which hold a high view of ordination, office tends to be identified with the right and duty of leadership. So whatever the respective spiritual gifts of the minister and other members of the congregation, the latter are generally (but in practice not always) willing to recognize that it is the task of the ordained to give leadership to the congregation. But in congregations holding a more charismatic understanding of gifts and therefore responsibility for ministry and service, there is inevitably and necessarily less distinction, in terms of ministry and service, between officeholders and others.

It remains a fact, however, that human groups, however loosely structured, cannot function without some kind of leadership and where there is a vacuum of leadership those with leadership gift will tend to fill it, consciously or unconsciously. Consequently, envy and resentment easily arise when individuals find that the congregation is looking to a person or persons other than themselves to take the lead in congregational life. In such a case, these resentments may be rationalized by arguing that the biblical principle of the multiplicity and dispersion of spiritual gifts implies that there is no need for leadership. Even where there is no such rationalization, the biblical principle can be held with great commitment so that the effect is identical.

Here, it is worth noting the distinction between 'ministry' and 'spiritual gift' on the one hand, and 'leadership' on the other, as they are frequently confused. Ministries and spiritual gifts are many and varied in character—see *Romans* 12:3–8, *1 Corinthians* 12 & 14, and *Ephesians* 4:7–16. Not all such gifts are leadership gifts, indeed, leadership is itself but one of the gifts (see *Romans* 12:8 (NIV)), and as argued earlier there is a limited group of gifts closely associated with it. So to argue against the need for leadership is to argue that certain gifts should not be exercised.

Moreover, despite the earlier references to the legitimacy of the principle of congregational leadership, it is worth dwelling on one aspect of it here, in the hope of clarifying understanding both of the functioning of charismatic gift and the need for responsible congregational leadership. A key term for understanding congregational life in the New Testament is that of fellowship (cf., *Acts 2:42*). Implicit in the term are the notions of partnership, sharing and common life. It was most obviously manifested in the early church in the sharing of goods and property (*Acts 4:32, 34–37*). Much else was shared, however, including grace and the work of the gospel (see *Philippians 2:5, 7*). The wide distribution of spiritual gift is itself a manifestation of this partnership, as is recognized by the reference in the traditional 'Grace' to the 'fellowship of the Holy Spirit'. In turn, all this reflects the partnership implicit in the biblical understanding of the Godhead.

But, notwithstanding this partnership, the equal standing of the Persons in the Godhead in no way implies that the Son and the Holy Spirit are not subordinate to the Father (see *1 Corinthians 3:23; 11:3; Hebrews 5:8*) or that initiative in the work of the Godhead does not flow from the Father (see, e.g., *John 5:17, 19–20, 30; Hebrews 5:4–5, 10*). Similarly, while we can rightly claim brotherhood with Christ as joint heirs with him (*Romans 8:17*), we nevertheless regard ourselves as those who are to follow him as disciples.

There is no reason for supposing that the church functions on a different basis and the New Testament is full of examples, not only of individuals who take the initiative in church life, but of the expectation that this ought to be the case (cf., *Timothy* and *Titus*). It is true that the notions of fellowship and partnership imply not hierarchy but group functioning and relatively loose structures in which each member has a similar standing. But it does not follow from that that each member of the group has precisely the same role, or that he or she is entirely autonomous (if the latter were so there would be no group and no fellowship). As leadership is an essential ingredient for effective group functioning, elders and congregations alike need to grasp that, with due respect to the wide exercise of gift, it is incumbent on the elders, in true servanthood and partnership with the congregation, to supply leadership to it, and to see that it is supplied in respect of all the groups and ministries within it.

This point has been laboured because it is all too easy, especially for a group leadership, to forget that it has a distinctive part to play. If it fails to provide that vital ingredient, the congregation will be the poorer for it.

The specifics of congregational leadership

It may assist understanding if the task of congregational
leadership is distinguished into a number of different strands.

First, there is *initiating* various ministries, activities and service[1]
within the congregation. Typically, this will require that, under the
Holy Spirit, the pastoral and other needs of the congregation
should be kept under review and opportunities for outreach and
community service should be considered, with the explicit purpose
of (1) identifying possibilities for ministry and service; (2) deciding
priorities; (3) identifying gift in the congregation to carry out those
possible ministries; (4) matching those gifts to the needs (it is
useless to initiate a ministry if the persons charged with it do not
have the appropriate spiritual gifts); and (5) commissioning
individuals or groups to undertake the chosen ministries (groups
should themselves be placed under clearly identified leadership).

In discharging this responsibility the elders should not forget
that initiative may come from others in the congregation rather
than from the elders themselves. In that case, the question will be
how the elders should respond to it—whether they encourage it,
or choke it without proper consideration. But it would be strange
if initiative never came from the recognized leaders of the
congregation.

Secondly, groups and individuals will need *guiding* and *directing*
in their various ministries. These functions have two aspects. Each
ministry, service and activity being undertaken in the congregation
should be monitored by the elders with the object of giving such
steering as appears necessary from time to time. This function
should not be neglected: Christian leaders can sometimes be
successful in initiating a work, but can then fail conspicuously in
taking any overt interest in it subsequently, so that the individual
or group concerned is left to struggle with the task apparently
forgotten. The initiative for discussion and review should not be
left with those undertaking the particular ministry, if only because
the first the elders may then hear of difficulties is likely to be the
despairing cry for help.

To ensure that the elders do not neglect any ministry, it may be
desirable that they should have arrangements for regular discussion
of each ministry with those who are undertaking it.

Beyond that, it is desirable that the elders should ensure that
those who undertake the various ministries should be properly
prepared and developed for their tasks; in particular, those who

lead key ministries, e.g., the leaders of house groups or of youth clubs, should be given specific training, either by the elders themselves or by someone brought in for the purpose.

Thirdly, the elders also *must* ensure that they give proper guidance and direction to *the congregation as a whole*. Too often congregations feel that their leaders are simply allowing things to drift aimlessly. Elders should review regularly the life of the congregation as a whole and all its ministries and gifts and consider in prayer its overall needs; and the coherence, relevance and effectiveness of its current ministries. They must, too, seek under God to look to the future and ask what are the fundamental matters which need attention and stimulation if the congregation is to make major progress in spiritual growth and evangelism. It would be salutary if from time to time the elders were to ask the Lord where he expects them to lead the flock in, say, the next five years. What are to be the objectives? What is the agenda for achieving them? What are the arrangements and structures needed?

The overall direction and guidance of the congregation in this way is a major task and it may be necessary for the elders to make special arrangements to discharge it, for example, by seeking the congregation's leave to go into retreat specifically in order to give the matter sustained prayer and discussion.

This task is often these days encapsulated in the word *vision*, and it certainly requires prophetic vision, which once received will need to be communicated effectively to the congregation. The need for such supernatural vision if a congregation is to grow healthily, and catch the responsibility to plant out further congregations, can hardly be over-estimated; nor the need for elders to seek it from the Lord himself. This strategic function is a fundamental obligation of eldership.

A fourth component of congregational leadership is that of *encouraging* the flock. Christian ministry and service are not easy. Even where regular arrangements are made for the review of activities, those leading them will be exposed to continual temptation to discouragement and despair, which are frequent methods by which Satan seeks to render Christian ministry ineffective. The elders need between them to retain close contact with all who undertake the various ministries of the congregation in order to be sure that nothing is wrong, to take an interest in the work, and to discharge the pastoral task of encouragement. Here, tact will be needed: it is important that, on the one hand, those concerned should feel that the elders care about them; and, on the other, that the impression should not be given that they are not to be trusted to do the job properly without constant monitoring.

Finally, congregational ministries may on occasion need *controlling*. Even in the best ordered congregation, things will go wrong and there may be disputes between individuals, or within and between groups, which will need to be regulated. Moreover, ministries and activities may need to be restructured. Some may need, with due pastoral care and tact, to be closed down as no longer serving useful spiritual and practical purposes—as sapping spiritual strength and growth rather than contributing to it (cf., *Ephesians 4:15–16*).

Properly undertaken, these tasks are by no means negligible, though unhappily they are frequently neglected. They bring into use in various ways the elder's tasks which have already been examined—those of pastoring, teaching and ruling. If they are to be summed up, it would be in a single word frequently used in other evangelical traditions in respect of the full-time congregational workers—that of *enabling* the congregation and each individual member to fulfil the various ministries and service to which the Lord has called them. 'Enabling' encapsulates the distinctive feature of Christian leadership which is missed whenever it is assumed that charismatic gift renders leadership unnecessary. For individuals look to others, and groups look to particular people within them, to supply a key attribute which they themselves lack, whatever their gifts. This is the ability to see what ought to be done and to cause it to happen, to help the group to get things done (including changing what is already going on). One brief definition of leadership is 'enabling other people to get things done, when otherwise they would not'. Without this function, gifts, for example, may go unused. It is an attribute which in the Christian context (and perhaps also in the non-Christian context) requires prophetic vision, including the ability to see possibilities in any particular set of circumstances which others cannot see. The Christian leader recognizes that to be truly effective this quality must be the work of the Holy Spirit, sought in prayer both alone and with fellow-leaders.

The special requirements of collective leadership

In western Europe and North America, there is a strong tradition of monarchical leadership. Against that background, many are inclined to argue that leadership within any group must, if it is to be effective, be concentrated in an individual. In the church, this view is reinforced by the incompetence of some collective leaderships and by the tradition in many denominations that congregational leadership should be concentrated in an individual who devotes his time wholly to the ministry. To those schooled in this tradition it is surprising to discover that the leadership of groups can be differentiated into a number of different functions which are normally discharged by different individuals within the leadership group (though one person may discharge them if insufficient suitable people are available in a particular group). The group leadership proposed in the New Testament recognizes this fact.

But as the inclination to monarchical leadership is so deeply embedded in the Anglo-Saxon consciousness, it is essential that the eldership should ensure that congregational leadership is not going by default and that the congregation is aware that it is not. The process by which effective collective leadership is forged and implemented is to be considered in the next chapter. Let it suffice here to stress that elders *must* above all find appropriate ways by which they can come to a common vision from the Lord for the congregation for which they are responsible. They *must* communicate that vision to it. They *must* give a united lead in the functions outlined above (cf., *Acts 6:2, 6; 11:27–30; 13:1–3; 15:6, 22–23, 30*). The eldership which cares for the spiritual and numerical growth of the congregation, and for the planting of further congregations, must see that it gets this right.

---

1. 'Ministry' and 'service' are used in the wide sense, as in *Romans 12* and *1 Corinthians 12*.

III

The Dynamics of Collective Leadership

8

THE EFFECTIVENESS OF THE ELDERSHIP GROUP

So far the main focus has been the elder as an individual. But throughout, the context has been that of plural eldership. The purpose now is to consider the vitally important question of how the elders of a congregation are to function effectively as a group if they are competently to discharge the onerous responsibilities which have been outlined so far. For however spiritual, competent and diligent elders may be as individuals, it is essential that any group holding and teaching plural eldership should function as *a coherent entity*, and be seen by the rest of the congregation to do so.

Unfortunately failure in this is all too easy, and the gap between the rhetoric and the reality has certainly led some to despair of the principle. Where there is failure, at best the result is a sense of vacuum of leadership; worse, that the elders convey to the church an uncertain sound to which it cannot rally; and worst, that individual elders, in appearance if not in fact, pull in contrary directions or even speak and work actively to frustrate their colleagues' intentions.

What follows focuses particularly on dysfunctional aspects of leaderships in churches of Brethren background. But, as team leadership becomes more and more the norm in evangelical local churches and para-church bodies, there may be considerably wider relevance. Fallen human beings cannot expect to find it easy to work in groups (see *Genesis* 4 and 11:1–9). There is among Christians, however, sometimes an over-optimism about what will be possible in redeemed people in this respect, and often a truly appalling lack of knowledge, both of self and of what is needed to make groups function effectively. Group or team leadership is not easy. Like marriage it requires commitment and hard work to make

83

it effective—which does not mean that it is not the New Testament norm. On the other hand, there is frequently found in Evangelicalism an individualism which will only tolerate monarchical leadership (albeit of a team) if it is exercised by that individual himself. The tendency is often exacerbated by the frequent sense of each individual that he or she has a direct personal line to God which authorizes the bypassing of structures of authority in the church. This is the source of much stress in local churches, and of the multiplication of independent works and para-church bodies giving expression to this unwillingness to accept the disciplines necessary for effective team or group action. Better group performance is often a crying need in many evangelical churches and para-church bodies.

Group dynamics

Ineffectiveness in group endeavour frequently stems from failure to understand how groups function and to understand the effects which the behaviour of each member can have on the functioning of the group as a whole. That such failures of understanding and practice should occur so extensively among Christian leaders is distressing, since the indwelling presence of the Holy Spirit is intended to confer love, peace, humility and unity (see *John 13–17 passim*) and to create a wholly distinctive partnership (fellowship) in common endeavour for the common good (see *1 Corinthians 12, Ephesians 4:1–16*). It is of course a prime purpose of Satan to neutralize this in order to frustrate the work of the Kingdom. This is why there is a special obligation upon elders to seek the Lord, and why others in the congregation need to support their elders particularly in prayer.

First, there is a number of points to be grasped under the general heading of *relationships within the eldership group*. It was noted in the preceding chapter that groups, however small, have a need for leadership, even if it is recognized only within the group itself. Such is human nature that there will therefore be temptations to jostle over position, status and power within the group. Where there is rivalry and concomitant suspicion between members (which will probably be perceived by the wider congregation), the group's ability to achieve its objectives and discharge its collective functions is bound to be impaired. And even distance between members of the group will reduce its effectiveness. It seems reasonable to suppose that the failure of the disciples to retain their coherence and solidarity behind Jesus in the face of his passion was in part attributable to the unworthiness of their ambitions (*Luke 22:24–27*).

For effective group behaviour, there need to be between elders strong and steady relationships founded upon (1) accurate self-knowledge and estimation; (2) knowledge of each other; (3) mutual recognition of each other's spiritual gifts and roles in the fellowship, and mutual encouragement in them; and (4) mutual trust.

Accurate *self-knowledge and estimation* is a component of personal Christian maturity which ought to characterize all who are called to eldership. Each elder needs a clear-eyed assessment of their own personal strengths, weaknesses and limitations, of their own gifts and of the roles to which individually they are fitted within the congregation. Without this, the functioning of the eldership can be expected to suffer, either because the individual is not doing the things within the group and the church which each ought to do, or because individuals are over-reaching themselves and trying to do things to which they ought not to aspire. This self-awareness is acquired, partly in private meditation upon scripture and in prayer, particularly confession, and partly in reflection upon the experience of personal interaction with others. It is a process of learning which should not stop upon becoming an elder: for only as responsibility is shouldered, and successes are recorded and mistakes made, are some of the most relevant characteristics brought into focus. There is here, too, a place for spiritual counsel and direction, both from fellow-elders and from others who may well have a clearer understanding of one's characteristics and performance than one has oneself.

Similarly, the necessary personal maturity of the elder should include a *sympathetic understanding and appreciation of colleagues*. While intimacy should characterize Christian fellowship, it does happen that individuals called to eldership are not well-known to the rest, and in any case the pressures of life and eldership can be such that even those working closely together can grow apart on the personal level. It is important that elders (and, I would recommend, their spouses) should give time, despite the press of other things, to prayer, fellowship and relaxation together, without the impediment of any agenda. The purpose is to build the bonds of love which should be evident to the congregation and which will survive the inevitable strains which responsibility imposes in an imperfect world.

Thirdly, each elder and the group as a whole should develop *an objective assessment and recognition of the gifts and optimum roles of each member of the group*. This done, each elder should feel free, and

should be *encouraged, to exercise these gifts and roles* without
constraint. It is in the nature of spiritual gifts that they are
variously bestowed; if the recipient does not, or is not permitted to,
exercise his or her own gifts, the body will be the poorer (1
Corinthians 12:4–7; 14–26). So it is a pity if, for fear of the
consequences for existing position, status or power, or simply by
neglect, the eldership group does not identify its various gifts,
assign to each member roles matching those gifts, and then set
each other free to discharge enthusiastically the tasks appropriate
to those roles.

Fourthly, and flowing to a great extent from the first three, the
elders need actively *to build trust between each other* in the fulfilling of
their individual roles. Each needs to be confident that if they play
their proper part, their colleagues will not be constantly carping, or
requiring them to give a detailed account of their actions, or requiring
them to justify them. There will be important matters of all kinds
which merit report to colleagues or prior discussion with them. But
an eldership will be ineffectual if action even in minutiae must
await collective discussion—where they may not even get settled!
The result is quite unnecessary delay. Where elders have confidence
in each other, both as to when they may take immediate action and
as to matters which should be reserved for discussion, unnecessary
inaction by committee will be avoided and the trumpet will give
a more certain sound. This trust is dependent on having mature
elders who know themselves and each other, who recognize and
encourage each other's gifts, and who have learned what teamwork
really means. This maturity includes the ability to accept and stand
behind the actions of colleagues even when those actions are not
quite as one would have done things oneself.

Leadership of the elders

Even where the principle of variety of gifts is held, its practical
implications for the *functioning of the eldership group* can fail to be
recognized. Just as the congregation is a group which needs
leadership (see the preceding chapter), so the elders themselves
form a group which itself needs leadership if it is to function
properly. And just as the leadership of the Holy Spirit is mediated
to the congregation through individuals, so leadership of the
eldership group will be mediated through individual members.

This is not to argue for monarchical leadership of the elders,
though there may be many circumstances in which practically a
great deal has come from one suitably-gifted elder. As noted in the

preceding chapter, distinct and different types of leadership function can be distinguished even in the smallest human groups, and they are frequently discharged by different individuals, each of whom might well be capable of discharging another of the functions in another group in which the distribution of abilities is different.

Failure to recognize the need for an individual or individuals to give a lead to the eldership can result in a form of paralysis within the group, so that it cannot perform its enabling function towards the congregation as a whole, because initiative within the elders is stifled or impaired and the group cannot command the confidence of the congregation. And since the group cannot in fact do without this initiating function, it is likely to emerge willy-nilly and to be given informal recognition by some of the members. If so, there is a ready stimulus to rivalry and discontent on the part of those unwilling to accept it. Such unwillingness to accept the need for individuals within the eldership to take a lead can threaten to turn the group into a perpetual experiment in dynamic tension, which saps emotional energy which ought to be devoted to the pastoral, teaching and enabling tasks. All this is relevant to the practical questions of chairmanship and secretaryship which will be considered in a moment.

In the most stable group of elders, role will still change slowly over time as the circumstances of individual elders and the congregation change. If the eldership is to function effectively, this fact must be recognized and faced openly so that the group can adapt to the change. This is never more important than when a new member joins, or when a prominent member dies or retires. Much time and energy can be wasted in absorbing the consequent dynamic changes in the group and adapting to a new balance of roles. It is wise to be aware of this phenomenon and to look to an orderly succession: the person leaving the group may have an important part to play in enabling the newly-shaped group to adapt itself to the changes.

Principles of collective behaviour

Some important principles of behaviour need to be observed if unnecessary tension is to be avoided and the coherence of the eldership is not to be undermined in fact or appearance. The first may be expressed as *consensus* on major issues and *agreement to differ* on minor ones. It is not practicable to suppose that upon major matters affecting the life and work of the congregation an eldership could proceed other than on the principle of substantial agreement, if not unanimity. Persistent disagreement in such matters would be bound to be debilitating to the elders and to threaten the credibility of their leadership.

In such matters, it is important that each elder should conduct themselves within the group with *integrity* and *openness*: in making clear to their colleagues their position and any reservations which they may have; and in avoiding any secret politicking with individual colleagues, or any appearance of it. Openness must be the watchword. Granted this, the elders must learn to handle their differences in an acceptable fashion: this requires patience and the willingness to spend time exploring them and the underlying reasons for them. Above all, time should be spent in prayer and perhaps fasting about them, in order to seek the mind of the Lord so as to establish a spiritually-inspired consensus among elders and congregation alike.

In lesser matters, it should be possible for individuals *to allow their preferences to be over-ridden by the majority* without feeling that some great personal or theological cause has been sacrificed. Nor should this impair the effectiveness and credibility of the group. But such a principle does call for discretion on the part of the elder concerned. There are strict limits within which it is possible on major and minor matters for the elder to make public dissent, especially if it is in a manner which casts doubt on the wisdom of colleagues. Plural eldership implies collective responsibility, which in turn implies solidarity with fellow-elders even when they are taking a course with which the individual may personally disagree. (Integrity may of course demand that, when members of the congregation ask about the matter, they should be referred discreetly to other elders for explanations.) If disagreement on important matters is persistent, it may be that the individual should consider resigning in order to avoid an ambiguous position.

Discretion in respect of personal and pastoral confidences is also essential. Such confidences can be expected to be shared between elders so that they will be better placed to pray and if necessary to agree on pastoral action. But the information simply cannot be for wider consumption, and to break such confidences is a serious indiscretion which calls into question both the elders' credibility and the suitability for eldership of the person concerned.

In this context, it is appropriate to refer to the difficult position in which elders' spouses find themselves. It is desirable that they should, so far as possible, share, at least in a passive way, in their partner's work, and there will be many matters of elders' business to which they will inevitably become privy. This however places upon them a considerable burden of discretion, which is why their credentials are relevant in the selection of elders. But there will be some matters, particularly pastoral confidences, which ought not to be shared by elders even with their spouses if the elders' claims to leadership of the congregation are not to be put at risk.

The mechanics of the eldership group

Thus far, this chapter has been concerned with principles, which will need to be applied sensitively in each particular set of circumstances. They are principles which seem to me to be relevant whenever people attempt group leadership, particularly in voluntary bodies with comparatively informal structures. No reference has been made to formal organisational structures. As further general principles, it may be stated that elders should seek to minimize such structures, to adapt them promptly to changing circumstances, and to avoid being dominated or bound by them. But this is not to suggest that some such structures are bad in principle: something is desirable if only to prevent the group from having regularly to re-invent various wheels to facilitate its operation. The suggestions made in the following paragraphs cannot be regarded as being of the same kind or on the same plane as the principles discussed in the first part of this chapter. They are no more than practical suggestions based on experience, but that experience suggests that they are likely to be desirable to varying degrees in virtually all circumstances.

Chairmanship

Practice with respect to chairmanship of the elders varies widely between Brethren congregations. No doubt, some appoint no one to steer meetings. Many appear to confine the chairman's role to the conduct of meetings; and rotate the responsibility widely from meeting to meeting, month to month, or year to year. No doubt, this reflects an anxiety not to accord too great a status to any individual, and not to impair the principle of group leadership. Insofar as such practices are followed it is my view that they need to be reconsidered.

It was stressed earlier that any group of elders needs leadership within itself and it is natural to associate that task with the task of chairmanship (others in the congregation inevitably do so). Moreover, any executive group needs a custodian of its decisions, whose responsibility is to pursue and co-ordinate action between meetings.

Whatever the practice, chairmanship should not in my judgement be imposed on those who do not have the necessary abilities to discharge it competently. It ought generally to be confined to those (probably two or at most three) members who are recognized as supplying leadership to the group. Moreover, such individuals need a proper opportunity to develop the role beneficially for the elders and the congregation, and ought therefore to carry the responsibility for a satisfactory period. It is an unwise, indeed counter-productive policy to rotate the task rapidly, simply in the name of preventing any individual elder from gaining a particular status. Not only is such a practice a negation of the principle of gift, but it may deny the person a position which would be for the good of the congregation.

While there is no need to use the title 'Chairman' or 'Chairperson' the arrangement ought to be made known to the congregation at large. They need to know to whom the elders look to perform this co-ordinating function. And they need to know to whom, with the secretary, they should address themselves at any time in order to raise with the elders both personal matters and general matters concerning the functioning of the congregation.

In my view, there are many congregations whose functioning would be improved at a stroke if reforms were made in this single area.

Secretaryship

The eldership is bound to need an individual to conduct a measure of the correspondence, to see to the convening of elders' meetings, to the preparation of agenda and the general ordering of elders' business in consultation with the chairman, and to the recording of discussion and decisions.

Meetings

The elders will need to meet regularly to discharge routine business and to consider normal pastoral matters. These meetings will need to be made known both to all the elders and to the congregation. In addition, there will be a need for meetings for prayer and to discuss special issues at greater leisure than would be possible in the regular meetings. In most cases, the fact of such special meetings can and should be made known to the congregation for their support in prayer. Meetings should not take place more frequently than is necessary (except those for prayer), and frequency will depend on the needs of the particular circumstances. But as has been observed earlier, the historical tendency seems to have been to give too little time to the onerous task of eldership.

Agenda

In most cases, unless the meeting is for prayer or to discuss one item which is known to all concerned, it is worth having an agenda prepared and circulated in advance. This has the advantage of concentrating the mind of chairman and secretary in advance as to what ought to be discussed at any particular meeting, and it may help elders to give advance thought and prayer to the matters for consideration.

Minutes

The habit of preparing minutes as a matter of record for reading at the next meeting dies hard, despite that fact that it was a practice imposed by the absence of simple and economical means of duplication. The photocopier produces a surplus of documents, but one advantage is that it permits prompt distribution of copies of minutes. In the normal case, they should be not so much a blow-by-blow account of the discussion but a summary of decisions, with details of responsibility for taking action upon them. Where necessary, the elders could draw in a non-member with suitable talents to discharge the task of producing accurate and prompt minutes: the position would itself be a useful way of preparing and training future elders.

Individual responsibility

Elderships may find it effective and useful to the execution of their leadership task, to place responsibility for particular areas of congregational life with particular elders. Their task would be to keep themselves fully informed about progress in the particular area assigned to them, to report to the elders, to act as a channel of communication between the elders and those carrying out the ministries concerned, and to resolve matters which do not need prior consideration by the elders.

Executive action

However dedicated elders may be, it will not be practicable for them to meet more than a few times each month. Even in spiritual matters there are a host of detailed questions which arise in normal congregational life from day to day which need to be settled without having to wait for collective consideration by the elders. If the mutual trust discussed earlier exists, some can be dealt with by individual elders; others can be decided by one or two members in consultation. But it may be desirable in some larger congregations for the elders to appoint a sub-group of 3 or 4 who can be available for half an hour each week to settle matters for executive action which could subsequently be reported to the elders as a whole if necessary.

As already indicated these are matters of practice rather than of principle, and still less of scriptural injunction. Precise arrangements on these lines need to be adjusted to the circumstances of each congregation and body of elders. But it is not sufficient for elders to have the right aspirations towards leadership, service, and spiritual and numerical growth in their congregations. They must show themselves capable of translating these aspirations into reality and of drawing their churches with them. The way in which the elders function as a body is crucial in achieving this objective.

---

1. There is a number of more or less complicated analyses by behavioural analysts of the different leadership functions required by groups. Professor Hunt distinguishes, for example, between the initiating task-leader role and the socio-emotional or maintenance role 'concerned with supportive responses, seeking consensus, resolving conflicts, and avoiding group disintegration'. (*Managing People at Work: A Manager's Guide to Behaviour in Organizations* (Pan Books, 1981) p. 84). His argument is that groups need both sorts of leadership if they are to function effectively.

9

THE ELDERS AND THE DEACONS

So far this volume has concentrated almost wholly upon the office
and tasks of the congregational elder. That has been deliberate and
stems from recognition of the practical importance that elders have
in the Brethren approach to church order and life; and from a belief
that it is essential to improve their spirituality and practical
performance if their congregations are to remain vital. *Inter alia,* the
argument has proposed a rather higher view of the authority and
task of the elder than is sometimes found in modern theology and
practice.

But there is no intention of proposing a new clericalism: if Milton
found that in the Puritan churches of his day new presbyter was
but old priest writ large, there is a danger—into which some
Charismatic groups as well as the Brethren have threatened to
fall—that elders who have sought to model themselves, as they
have thought, more closely on the New Testament will outstrip
both presbyter and priest in arrogating to themselves both
authority and spiritual function.

Lest we seem to fall into that danger, it is time to redress the
balance and consider, first, the role and relationship of the elders
to other congregational officeholders envisaged in the New
Testament; and, then, the role of the rest of the congregation and
the elders' accountability to them.

Recent trends

Generalisations about practice in any group of Protestant congregations is risky. But two main developments in church order in

Brethren churches in the last generation are discernible. First, beginning in the mid 1960s, the larger churches progressively appointed groups, distinct from the elders, under the title of deacon. Secondly, and more recently, congregations both large and small have moved towards the appointment of individuals supported by the congregation to work within it on a full-time or part-time basis.

The mode of appointment of those bearing the title of deacon has varied: some churches have followed the practice of *Acts 6:1–7* and have chosen by election by church members. Others no doubt have followed the customary practice of selection by the elders.

The tasks of those thus appointed has probably varied rather less. In most places they seem to have been given responsibility for the maintenance of fabric, equipment and transport; for seeing that various housekeeping tasks are properly and regularly discharged, e.g. cleaning and preparation of rooms for meetings; and, in some places at least, for the administration of finances and the associated book-keeping. Originally, most deacons will have been men, but in my own church in recent years the office has been open to women and no doubt in other churches there has been a similar development. But in few churches do women seem to have been given any formal pastoral and practical position similar to that widely held to be described in *1 Timothy 3:5, 9, 10* (in respect of which it has been suggested that there was in the early church a third office—of widow—parallel to that of elder and deacon).[1]

The need for assistance for the elders

There are good reasons why elders should have been concerned to delegate to others the practical tasks which derive to a large extent from the ownership of buildings specifically for use by the congregation. Where the sense of ownership is diffuse, it is essential that responsibility for maintenance should be allocated clearly to one or more individuals. Buildings do have to be kept in order and be prepared satisfactorily for use by various groups in the congregation. Where there is no allocation of responsibility separate from the elders, they will naturally be called to account by the congregation. The consequence is that the elders' time can easily be eaten up by discussion of practical details and even by repairing and cleaning buildings, setting out chairs, and maintaining vehicles. It is not, of course, that any elder should regard any of these tasks as being beneath them. When necessary, the congregation does need to be set the example of seeing that their elders are willing to take off their jackets for menial tasks. But a congregation is also very foolish if it expects its elders to engage in these tasks to the exclusion of their prime spiritual functions; and elders are equally foolish if they allow this to happen. The elders *must* make sure that they concentrate their attention on the spiritual tasks which have been analysed earlier (*Acts 6:2–4*).

But to warn elders against entangling themselves in these practical details is to put the point negatively. More positively, they need to make sure that they receive assistance where possible with their spiritual tasks, too. The elders will only be a small number of the congregation. Even if they can devote themselves part-time or full-time to the work, their resources of time will be limited. Their responsibilities as already outlined are daunting. We shall consider this point in more detail in the next chapter, but the New Testament is unequivocal that they will be far from exclusively the repository of spiritual gift in the church. One of their prime tasks is to encourage, lead and organize other significant spiritual gifts in the congregation.

Elders are, however, the possessors of power in the congregation. They remain tainted by sin and unhappily it is in the nature of fallen human beings that having acquired power they readily succumb to the temptation to hoard it and preserve it, rather than sharing it in a manner consistent with the scriptural principle of fellowship. Elders can be deeply defensive about allowing others to do minor things in the congregation, let alone the more spiritual, more *prominent* and more *acclaimed* tasks in the church. This attitude is deeply repugnant to the doctrine of spiritual gift in the New Testament (see *1 Corinthians 12:22–25*). The elders should not be afraid to encourage others to assist them with pastoral work, to lead home groups for Bible study and prayer (though the elders may find it convenient to make these groups the basis of their pastoral organization and therefore to be closely concerned with them), and to teach young Christians the basics of the faith.

The role of the deacon

The office of deacon is potentially a subject for detailed consideration in itself, and the role and tasks do require to be teased out from the New Testament. It can in fact be questioned how far Brethren and to some extent Baptist congregations may have missed the point in relating the office largely to the practical tasks

of the maintenance of fabric, etc. The other Baptist tradition in
which the deacons are the senior 'lay' assistants, counsellors, and
permanent representatives of the congregation alongside the
minister (who is best considered as analogous to a single elder) is
in this nearer to the scriptural concept, perhaps.

This is not to argue that practical tasks do not have to be done
with commitment and in the spiritual manner required of every
believer; and financial matters need to be in the hands of persons
of maturity and probity. But it is beyond question from scripture
that deacons are to be people of the highest spiritual calibre: the
qualifications outlined in *1 Timothy 3:8–13* are comparable with
those required of elders, save that the elder must in addition be
qualified as a teacher; and, if *Acts 6:1–6* refers to the appointment of
deacons,[2] the condition imposed by the apostles on the electoral
process was that those chosen should be 'of good repute, full of the
spirit and of wisdom' (*Acts 6:3*). Of these, Stephen ('a man full of
faith and of the Holy Spirit' even at the time of his appointment—
Acts 6:5) and Philip certainly emerged within a short time as men of
great spiritual stature.

The deacon was a person who approached the spiritual qualities
of the apostles, let alone the elder. It does not therefore seem to
make sense to confine the deacon's role to minor matters of
practical organization. As to the vexed question of role, the
designation of the office ('servant') offers a clue when compared
with the task in *Acts 6* of supervising and meeting the wants of
those in material need in the congregation and doing so from the
financial provision made by the congregation as a whole. In effect,
they were placed in the same position as Judas with respect to the
Twelve—they had charge of and administered the money set aside
for the relief of the poor both within the congregation and outside
it (*John 12:4–8* and *13:29*). This suggests that the centre of gravity of
the deacon's ministry is intended to be that of seeing to the
practical needs of *people* within and outside the church and that the
primary spiritual gifts that they require are those set out in *Romans
12:7–8:* 'service'; 'contribution'; 'giving aid';[3] and 'doing acts of
mercy'; and in *1 Corinthians 12:28:* 'gifts of support'[4]—'helper' in
the RSV.

The reference to women in *1 Timothy 3:11* is almost certainly to
women deacons (n.b. not deaconesses) and Paul was probably
using the term in a technical sense when he described Phoebe as a
deacon (n.b., not deaconess) of the church at Cenchreae (*Romans
16:1*). This implies that the office, tasks and gifts of deacon were
even in New Testament times shared on equal standing by men

and women. The high spiritual character and tasks of those formally enrolled as widows are even less in doubt: 'She . . . has set her hope on God and continues in supplications and prayers night and day; . . . she must be well attested for her good deeds, as one who has brought up children, shown hospitality, washed the feet of the saints, relieved the afflicted, and devoted herself to doing good in every way'[5] (*1 Timothy 5:5–10*).

All this leaves little room for doubt that those holding these offices were to assist the elders by giving help primarily of a practical and material kind to those in need. But experience shows that there is a fine and unclear line between practical and pastoral and spiritual help—certainly widows in the early church were expected to have a teaching role among younger women, including preparation for baptism. Hence the need for the work to be done by those of true spirituality who shared the love of Christ towards those in need (cf., the juxtaposition in *Romans 12* of vv.7–8 and 9–10).

Here is a major role which regrettably is often hopelessly neglected in many evangelical churches in the west, including those of Brethren origins. The congregations concerned are much the poorer for it in two ways.

First, the body is weakened in itself. For the neglect of practical help towards needy members of all ages marches closely with the neglect of pastoral care on the spiritual side. It is scarcely surprising that those in need feel that no-one cares for them in the church and that there is often more help to be had from non-Christians. In consequence, the sheep melt away to be scattered in the world.

Secondly, there are consequences for evangelism. For those outside the church are denied the example of love and care which they ought to see among Christians; nor are they themselves touched directly by that care. By the authority of Christ, the natural constituency in evangelism is the poor, the captive, the blind and the oppressed (*Luke 4:18*). If the office, tasks and gifts just described are not in evidence, it is not surprising that this constituency remains unimpressed. It is interesting that where the Spirit moves in genuine revival, this gap is usually filled and momentum is added to the movement. Where the gap exists, it is evidence of spiritual decline and death. If such a gap exists in a local congregation, the responsibility must ultimately lie with the elders' failure to teach about the need for these ministries, to encourage the church in the relevant gifts, to encourage the church to appoint suitable people to the offices concerned, and to set the individuals free to do their proper work.

The elders' relationship to the deacons

On this analysis, the main spiritual and practical care of the church should rest with a group wider than simply the elders; elders, deacons and other senior women should each be contributing to the care of the church according to their proper gifts. In the smaller congregation, for example, this group might well comprise no more than two or at most three elders, a deacon or two (elected by the congregation?) and two senior women (who might or might not be recognized as deacons, or even in my view as elders, according to circumstance).[6] The boundaries between the spheres of operation of the three types of person might be comparatively ill-defined, except that authority and the main teaching burden would lie with the elders in the group. There is no reason why on many occasions the traditional meeting for oversight should not include all these types. In the larger church, however, it might well be more convenient to define the organizational arrangements more clearly, though there would still have to be provision for close working.

In either case, other reliable individuals will be needed, possibly led by a deacon, to attend to practical tasks relating to buildings, equipment and book-keeping. But these responsibilities and those of deacons should not be confused: the deacons should not be distracted from their proper tasks, any more than should the elders.

Despite the authority, rule and leadership of the elders, there should, too, be a real effort to avoid a hierarchical relationship between the elders, the deacons and other senior people, and those doing practical tasks. The organizational thought forms within which we tend automatically to think in the west do not harmonize well with the New Testament concept of gift. It is easy to think of the deacons as being responsible and accountable to the elders in detail for their stewardship. The elders do have the authority to intervene on occasion when things are going badly wrong. But election by the congregation (if that is the practice) implies in fact responsibility and accountability to them rather than to the elders, especially in the use of funds which the congregation has provided to meet practical need.

Separation of powers rather than hierarchical relationship seems a better model for helping us to understand the relationship intended by scripture. Elders and deacons each have their proper sphere of activity according to their gifts, and the responsibility of each is to the Lord and the congregation more than it is to each other. There may be occasions on which it is for the elders to come cap in hand to the deacons rather than vice versa, e.g. if they have in mind some project which requires the financial support of the congregation. For their part the deacons need to get on with their proper tasks without feeling a constant need to refer to the elders for approval.

This assessment of the day-to-day functioning, organization and relationships of elders, deacons and other senior people with spiritual gifts may seem strange to those educated in a tradition of organizational tidiness. But the body of Christ is intended to be a living organism, infused by the Holy Spirit, bursting with life. Untidinesses and asymmetries are often characteristic of that life. It is cold rationalism which has the opposite characteristics: there is still too much of it about in the church.

---

1. See W. Hendriksen, *Commentary on I & II Timothy and Titus* (London: Banner of Truth Trust, 1959) p. 173; and A. Kuen, *Ministères dans l'église* (St. Légier: Editions Emmaüs, 1983) p. 73.

2. The text does not in fact describe the seven as deacons.

3. 'More probably it stands for "the administrator in charge of the charitable work of the congregation" (Cranfield: RSV agrees).' *The New Bible Commentary Revised* (London Inter-Varsity Press, 1970) p. 1040.

4. C. K. Barrett's rendering, which 'must be to some extent a guess, but the word is used, notably in papyri referring to the Ptolemies, of defence or succour given by a higher authority.'—*A Commentary on the First Epistle to the Corinthians*, 2nd edition (London: Adam and Charles Black, 1971) p. 295.

5. I doubt whether now the emphasis in relation to this passage should be on widowhood as such. The context makes plain that the requirement is for those of high spiritual standing and appropriate gifts who are in a position to give single-minded and permanent service to Christ, free from e.g. family obligations.

6. The figures are simply illustrative.

10

THE ELDERS AND (THE REST OF) THE CONGREGATION

By focusing on the role and position of the deacons and other senior people in the congregation, the last chapter sought to redress somewhat the imbalance resulting from the earlier concentration on the role of the elder. But the elders and deacons will normally account for only a small quantum of the members of a local church—the thousands of Christians in Jerusalem in the earliest days of the church were perhaps untypical because so many of them were by definition novices, but for a considerable period authority lay in the hands of twelve apostles, seven deacons and an indeterminate number of elders (cf., *Acts 15:6, 22*). There is something seriously wrong with a congregation which comprises many chiefs and few Indians. So a consideration of role and tasks of the elder would be incomplete without examining the elders' (and the deacons') relationship with (the rest of) the flock and the rights of that flock.

The relationship between elders and congregation

It would be fair to say, I think, that the traditional attitude of Brethren elders towards their congregation has been in essence authoritarian. The tendency has been to emphasize that the elder's status is derived from appointment by God, through the medium of the existing eldership; and that the elder has a right to rule and the duty of oversight, while the congregation for its part has a duty of submission to its elders. The relationship has in consequence tended to be understood as one-way in character: church member and congregation owe obedience to the elders, and the latter's obligation, if any, is simply to make clear their requirements to the

101

flock. There is often little sense of accountability to the congregation for the elders' stewardship, or even of obligation to explain and justify their decisions and policies. In the extreme case, the approach could simply be described as dictatorial. (The same kind of approach can be found among other Christian leaderships.)

For its part, the rest of the congregation has tended traditionally to adopt an ambivalent or oscillating attitude towards the eldership. Often, the dominant attitude towards the elders' authority is of acquiesence, ranging from philosophical to quietly grumbling in character. This can on occasion, however, be punctuated by an individualism, frequently born of sheer frustration, in which individuals and groups take virtually unilateral action in church matters, especially in spheres in which they can claim that some degree of responsibility has been accorded to them. It is not uncommon to find that some initiative or other has been taken without any reference to anyone in the congregation, let alone to the elders.

To a degree this is caricature. But it is recognizable and, it may be argued, far removed from the relationship between elder and congregation proposed in the New Testament. There, despite the clear authority of the elder as described earlier, we can see the dual lines of responsibility already suggested in the discussion of the relationship between elders and deacons. Where the latter are elected, the line of responsibility to the congregation is clearer. But even in the absence of election, the primary calling, as perceived in scripture, of both the elder and the deacon is to servanthood: in that status they are servants *both* of God *and* of the congregation. It may therefore legitimately be argued that, as with all servants, they are responsible and accountable[1] to their masters—in this case, both God and the congregation. Indeed, the focus of the Lord's teaching and example on the servant status of the Christian leader is more on service, and therefore responsibility, to brother and sister in the family of God than it is on the obligation to serve God (see *Luke 22:26, John 13:14–16*).

This biblical relationship is brought more sharply into focus by considering the high position accorded in scripture to the congregation itself. Despite the existence of priestly and Levitical castes, and later of kings, that position can already be perceived in shadow in the Old Testament. The old covenant was with people rather than simply with leaders and under it a certain egalitarianism can be perceived in the relation between people and their covenant God: the superior status, as distinct from authority, later accorded to the monarch in Israel obviously derived from the hardness of the people's heart rather than the primitive purpose of God (see *1 Samuel 8:10–18; Hosea 8:4, 13–14*).

The promise is comprehensively fulfilled in the New Testament. There we see a new covenant with a new people which embraces the youngest to the oldest. All receive the sign and guarantee of the covenant—the Holy Spirit; from that Spirit all have knowledge of God and all have the heart of flesh to obey God; all are kings and priests to God; and each receives (from young to old) spiritual gifts, severally according to the will of God, for the mutual upbuilding of the church. The old Israel was dependent usually on a few leaders; in the new, spiritual insight, spiritual power, spiritual character and spiritual standing are now much more widely disseminated through the whole body.

Consistent with this teaching, the New Testament accords a much higher status and role to the congregation at large than has often been accepted and practised in the experience of the church—though it should be noted that in times of revival and renewal there has been a constant tendency to rectify matters. The account of the council at Jerusalem in *Acts 15* is noteworthy in this context. The church as a whole at Antioch was associated with the request that initiated the council (*v.5*); it was the church at Jerusalem which welcomed the (numerous) delegates from Antioch (*v.4*—on delegates, see *v.2*); the judgement of the assembly of apostles and elders (*vv.6, 12*) was ratified by the acclaim of the whole church, who were associated with the selection of messengers from them to the church at Antioch; and it was the whole congregation in Antioch who were the addressees of the letter from the Jerusalem church and its recipients on its arrival (*vv.23, 30*). This pattern is followed not only in respect of the Pauline letters, which apart from the understandable exceptions of those to Timothy, Titus and Philemon, were addressed to the whole church (*n.b.*, the order in *Philippians 1:1*, 'To all the saints in Christ Jesus who are at Philippi, with the bishops and deacons'). It is followed also in the case of the prophetic messages to the seven churches in *Revelation 2 and 3*— they were to the messenger of *the church* in each case. As was noted in considering the rule of the elder, the duty of excommunication is laid on the whole Corinthian church, not simply the elders (*1 Corinthians 5:4–5*; and *2 Corinthians 2:6*).

The rights of the congregation

This teaching has important implications for the elders' attitude towards the congregation. First, it follows that the elders cannot, individually or collectively, regard themselves as spiritually superior to the congregation. Their position as elders gives them duties and obligations towards it and only rather limited rights in respect of it. Secondly, the elders are not to domineer over those in their charge (*1 Peter 5:4*): they dare not treat them in the dictatorial and authoritarian fashion which is sometimes reported of elders both in the Brethren and in other church connexions. Despite the pastoral metaphor, the congregation cannot be regarded as mere sheep in the derogatory sense of the word, or as simple pawns in the spiritual battle, or as children who are incapable of understanding and participating in serious family discussions. Rather, there is an obligation on the elders to seek to take the congregation into their confidence on all matters of significance which affect the congregation as a whole (though, of course, personal pastoral matters are to be kept within the strict confidence of the elders except *in extremis*).

This is not simply a matter of principle, but also of practicality. The aim of the elders in their leadership of the congregation should be to seek a unity of life and purpose which comes from God, the one heart and one soul which the Jerusalem church experienced as recorded in *Acts 4:32* and which Paul enjoined in *Ephesians 4:2–3*. It is that which renders the congregation a powerful and united force for God in its common ministry. This is not likely to be achieved unless the elders recognize the high spiritual standing which the whole congregation enjoys before God.

Thirdly, in the light of the New Testament's teaching on the nature, diversity and distribution of spiritual gifts and experience, the elders dare not regard themselves as the sole repository of knowledge, wisdom, vision, ability and resources for action within the congregation. Despite the magnitude of the elders' duties and responsibilities, they must not come to think of themselves as a new priestly caste which is alone entitled to undertake the spiritual and prestigious ministries in the church. Confidence in the congregation as a whole must extend to confidence in individual members to carry out the spiritual ministries to which they are fitted by the spiritual gifts which God has chosen to give. The elders' role is to pastor, to teach, to support, to initiate, to guide, to inspire, to lead, to encourage and to liberate for service. It is certainly not to hobble, to contain and to monitor officiously except where it is patently necessary to do so. Accordingly, the elders should wish to make free use of others in the congregation who have something to contribute to the ministry of the church. Indeed, it is the congregation's right to exercise that ministry.

Building the relationship

It should go virtually without saying that, on the elder's side, the key to a satisfactory relationship with ordinary church members is a proper estimation of their own status and that of the congregation, and of their obligations towards the congregation. Where there is a right attitude, the practical aspects of the relationship can be expected to fall out satisfactorily according to the particular circumstances.

Good communications

These are essential. Many of the problems of churches (and other organisations) can be traced to poor communications between leaders and the rest of the church. It is worth investing a lot of effort in correcting this fault.

The eldership must avoid either being, or appearing to be, a remote body which is uninterested in the feelings, ideas and aspirations of the congregation. It should not consider that it can simply hand down its views from on high. It must be in constant and close touch with the members and ensure that that communication is two-way in character. The congregation need not only to be kept abreast of the elders' thinking and plans, but to be sure that their own views are heard and carefully weighed, even if ultimately they have to be set on one side.

Often this two-way communication can be informal. Elders must seek regular fellowship, socially and on specific occasions, with the flock, and ensure that no member is excluded from that fellowship (for this purpose some degree of organization and system may be necessary in the larger church). These occasions should not be wasted. Unobtrusively, the elder should be listening carefully to what each member has to say. Many will not be slow to make their views known about congregational life; others will need some tactful stimulation to unburden themselves. Discreetly, the elder should seek consciously to sound out the members' views on issues of the moment and to convey the elders' thinking on them as necessary. Regular pastoral visitation and conversations also present opportunities which can be used for similar purposes. It is surprising however how poor some elders can be at informing themselves about what is in the mind of the congregation.

Consultation

There will also be a need for more formal communication with the congregation. Sometimes, this will legitimately be of a one-way character. In virtually all churches of all denominations, this is one function of the weekly notices, and of the introduction to prayer sessions and meetings. But it is surprising in how many churches these opportunities are squandered by allowing the task to be discharged by poor communicators, or by people who have no conception of the importance of these opportunities to the effective functioning of the congregation, and of the need to use them to encourage members in various ministries and activities. Where it is feasible for oral notices to be supplemented by a weekly or monthly bulletin, or both, it is essential that these should be well produced and that the elders should grasp them as additional means of communicating with the congregation, especially where the messages need to be precise or to be repeated by way of *aide-mémoire*.

But formal communication will sometimes need to be two-way, i.e. consultative, because the views of the congregation need to be sought. On occasion, written communication will be helpful and desirable; sometimes short and intelligible questionnaires may be useful. But many church members find writing tedious, and meetings will frequently be a more effective means of consulting them. The meeting of church members is an obvious mechanism. Traditionally, in Brethren churches (except those actually governed by a church meeting), such meetings have been infrequent (say, twice a year) and have been used principally for report and communication rather than consultation. But increasingly my impression is that they are used for consultative purposes as well. Many churches would benefit if this practice were more widespread. The experience of many lively and growing fellowships is that more frequent meetings of church members are desirable in order to keep the elders in close touch with the members and the members in close touch with the various ministries of the church for the purposes of prayer and practical help. There may be a tendency to think that such meetings are less useful than those for, say, teaching but, where they are combined with prayer, they may well repay the time invested in them.

To be effective, church meetings should be carefully planned by the elders. They need adroit chairmanship if the congregation is not to form a poor view of the elders' competence. They must therefore ensure that this task is entrusted to a suitably gifted person—again no Buggins' turn, please! But it must also be recognized that such formal and possibly large meetings give the edge to the confident and articulate members who may not be particularly representative of the church as a whole. The elders must make sure that they are in touch with a wide cross-section of the congregation on major issues. Where it has a system of house or area fellowship groups, they will often provide an effective network of consultation, in which the elder or elders responsible for the group can initiate an informal discussion of important matters in an atmosphere in which the diffident member may more easily express his or her views. Such a mechanism should also be supplemented by one-to-one discussion if that is the only way to elicit the views of the individual concerned.

Decision-making

The purpose of consultation is not of course to take a simple referendum of congregational opinion; and still less is it to decide issues by head-counting. It is to inform the elders so that they may, in conjunction with the deacons where appropriate, reach sensible conclusions under the guidance of the Holy Spirit. But the nature of a Christian congregation is such that the elders do need to elicit the whole-hearted support of the congregation for their decisions and leadership. Churches are in essence voluntary societies and elders cannot expect to be able simply to issue orders to be obeyed as in a military formation. Nor is it plausible on grounds of scripture or of reason to expect people to make irredeemable vows to submit themselves to the elders, come what may. That does not seem consistent with the status accorded to the congregation in scripture; and fallen people will in any case find it hard, whatever vows they have made, to submit to an authoritarian leadership if they doubt its spiritual credentials, or rationality, or competence, or all three. There is therefore no alternative to enlisting the consent of the congregation on major issues.

This will often require careful and effective communication and consultation, both before and after the decision, in order to win the confidence of the congregation and to convey the necessary vision. And on occasion, it may be perfectly consistent with scriptural principle for the elders to leave a decision to the congregation either by establishing the consensus or by a vote (matters requiring the congregation's full-hearted financial support or deep personal commitment of time by each member might well fall into this category).

In admitting the congregation to decision-making in these matters, the elders need not feel that they are in any way jeopardizing their God-given authority as shepherds of the flock of God. The aim is to secure that under God the congregation is indeed of one heart and one soul.

---

1. I distinguish accountability from responsibility in so far as the former suggests a more detailed and stringent obligation to explain stewardship.

IV

Education for Eldership

11

PREPARATION AND DEVELOPMENT OF ELDERS

In defence of educating elders

Among those whose understanding of Christian ministry is essentially charismatic in the biblical sense, it is common to find a strong antipathy to the suggestion that individuals should have formal training for responsibility in the church. This view can be traced to a number of troubling ideas.

First, it seems to be held that unless a word or action is spontaneously and *immediately* inspired by the Holy Spirit, to the virtual elimination of forethought, it cannot be regarded as being truly, or at least in the best sense, spiritual. Thus, there can be much suspicion if a preacher has clearly spent much time in preparation for a particular event, or if he is too obviously assisted by prepared notes. The application of this idea to eldership is that the spiritual elder will simply *know* what to do and how to do it in any particular circumstances. Moreover, the idea of immediate reception of spiritual light can undermine the concept that there is anything to be learned from others, a view which may easily be reinforced by simple human pride.

Secondly, it is commonly feared that formal education and training will inevitably imply intellectualism—the inculcation of mere theories and facts which have little to do with spiritual life, which may indeed be anti-spiritual, and which will certainly be of no real assistance with Christian service and responsibilities.

Thirdly, there is the related concern that training will comprise mainly the teaching of various secular and practical techniques which will prove to be a carnal resource rather than the spiritual resource which can alone be profitable in Christian work. Consequently, there is deep suspicion of the language and concepts of secular leadership and management: objectives, performance, organization, planning, effectiveness, etc.

Fourthly, insensitivity to the need for preparation and development for eldership can be traced to the view of eldership discussed in chapter 3. For if eldership is no more than a status (with no distinctive duties) and involves only the recognition of work which the individual concerned is already carrying out in the congregation, it follows that, insofar as there are tasks to be discharged, those becoming elders are already carrying them out satisfactorily and no action to improve performance is desirable or necessary.

Fifthly, there is the related consideration that, since so little thought needs to be given to the duties and tasks of the elder, there need be no questioning of how they ought to be done, nor of how shortcomings might be remedied.

Some of these attitudes have at root a grain of truth. Specific preparation is not an essential precondition of powerful preaching; and extensive intellectual knowledge of scripture and theology will avail the preacher nothing unless he has encountered God and has a word from him for the occasion in question. Our arrangements for worship and ministry should accord an appropriate opportunity for spontaneous words from the LORD. There is a place, too, in eldership for the word of knowledge of *1 Corinthians 12:8*. Moreover, secular techniques on their own cannot build the true church. Most great movements of the Spirit have spawned educational and theological establishments which in due course have been in the van of heresy and infidelity—though it would be interesting to ask whether these phenomena are as much the cause of spiritual decline as its symptom. Finally, all the education in the world will not make someone a better elder if they should not be one anyway, because they do not have the necessary spiritual gifts and calling.

But even when these grains of truth are granted, the consequent attitudes suggest a questionable understanding of scripture in two ways. At the fundamental level, they seem to suggest a misunderstanding of the relationship between the flesh and the spirit after the Holy Spirit has come to indwell the believer. At a simpler level, they seem to ignore the vast evidence of scripture for the preparation and training of individuals and groups for the work of God.

There is a subtle point to be grasped here. The coming of the Spirit does not obliterate the flesh: he intends to transform it radically in sanctification. Paul tells us in *1 Corinthians 1 and 2* that God has made foolish the wisdom of the world (*1:20*); rejects plausible words of wisdom (2:10); and stresses the revelation of the Spirit (2:10). He also explained to the Philippians that he counted his former life and education loss for the sake of Christ (3:7). Yet *Acts* and Paul's epistles bear evidence throughout of his effective use of the knowledge derived from that education both for the purposes of the gospel and for building the church (cf., his preaching to the synagogue at Pisidian Antioch (*Acts 13:16–41*) and at the Areopagus in Athens (*Acts 17:23–31*)). Moreover, even if Paul's education before his conversion were to be set aside, it would be necessary to note the long period of preparation for his ministry after he was converted, both intensively in the Arabian experience and subsequently, it appears, in Tarsus, before he came into prominence in the church. It is clear that Timothy's (and others') journeyings with him were an apprenticeship in church planting and care. Yet notwithstanding the benefit of that, Paul thought it wise to send him what amounted to two manuals in congregational ministry for his guidance. Turning to the Old Testament, we have only to consider the lengthy and varied preparation of, e.g., Moses, Joshua, Samuel and David, to understand the importance given by scripture to training for service—which included in some cases a secular and practical training (in Moses, for example, the LORD wasted neither the 40 years spent in Pharoah's court nor the 40 years as a shepherd in Sinai). Finally, there is the example of Jesus's three-year preparation of the disciples.

In the face of all this biblical evidence, the frequent neglect and even rejection in Brethren circles of the training of elders is mystifying.

A broad preparation

If the principle is accepted, what kind of preparation and training is needed? Much Christian education, even that designed for those who are to enter full-time Christian ministry, tends to focus rather narrowly on doctrinal and theological knowledge. This is perhaps understandable in the case of young students whose level of biblical knowledge and understanding needs to be raised rapidly to equip them for full-time ministry—though I suspect there is a need for a radical review of the curricula and basis of staffing of theological and Bible colleges in Europe and north America in the light of the rising average age of students and the work that they are likely to be doing when they complete their courses. Those selected for congregational eldership can be expected to be mature and should not have been considered suitable for eldership unless they were already giving evidence of a thorough grasp of scripture. Further, the traditional regard for scripture in Brethren circles tends still to ensure that elders have some proficiency in doctrinal matters (though it should not be taken for granted and the tradition may not be as healthy as it was).

None of this implies that biblical and doctrinal understanding is unimportant: in particular, where elders have been brought up, perhaps unconsciously, in a particular rigid scheme of interpretation, it may be desirable that their horizons should be widened somewhat. Biblical studies will also have their place in the preparation of younger people with eldership potential. And elders should not imagine that they can draw down their scriptural capital over a long period without unfortunate consequences for their ministry. They must ensure that their private devotions give adequate time to the study of scripture in depth, and it would be salutary if from time to time they were to attend, say, a week's summer school which concentrates on biblical material.

This chapter is, however, concerned with the education and training of those who are *already* elders, and for them the priorities lie elsewhere, in my judgement. The first and most important priority in the training of most existing elders is pastoral care. It is common for people to become elders in Brethren congregations with very little idea or experience of how to undertake routine pastoral matters (e.g., visitation and preparation for marriage), or of how to approach the more serious pastoral problems, e.g., marital break-down; helping the dying and the bereaved; mental breakdown which may or may not be closely associated with spiritual problems; and the influence of the demonic.

Secondly, there are the mechanics and content of basic instruction in the faith: nurturing new disciples and preparation for baptism.

Thirdly, there is understanding of the dynamics of leadership and of congregational life, i.e., how churches function as human groups, and the distinctive contribution which the elders can make as leaders to enable the congregation to function more effectively—to be a church in the biblical sense.

Fourthly, there is a need for elders to understand better their role and task of giving strategic guidance to the congregation. On what basis should its present condition and activities be evaluated, and how and in what direction is the congregation to be moved forward in order to fulfil God's purposes for it? Here, there is an important related requirement: elders need some knowledge of trends and developments in congregational life, not only in similar congregations in this country, but in other denominations and abroad. Though frequently despised in Brethren circles, there is an important place for learning from others and applying their experience in our circumstances (as a matter of fact, in congregational life, there is very little true originality; we are often experimenting with the ideas of others).

Continuing education

Generally in Brethren congregations, little provision seems to be made for the preparation and training of elders, even by trying to give suitable experience to those about to be invited to share in oversight. For those just coming into eldership, there would be advantage in a period of intensive instruction. But any initial preparation of this kind should not be regarded as imparting all that is needed. Those who have already been elders for a long period would often say that the whole process has been one of learning by experience (perhaps even to the misfortune of those in their care!), and no elder should consider himself beyond learning, and beyond identifying weaknesses and lack of understanding which affect performance as an elder. The passage of time will itself reveal important gaps in knowledge and understanding, and the elder, however old and experienced, ought to keep on the lookout for relevant opportunities to fill such gaps. It is a serious matter when an elder no longer has the mental and spiritual elasticity to see the need to learn new things which would improve performance.

Opportunities and methods

Many congregational elders are in full-time secular employment. Their opportunities for extended periods of education are limited. This has its disadvantages. But often their secular work will give them relevant experience not necessarily available to full-time Christian workers: those in positions of responsibility are often required to attend training courses which include material which, with suitable transpositions and testing against scripture, can be applied in eldership, e.g., material on group behaviour, leadership and presentational skills. In most cases, however, the elder's preparation and training must be developed gradually, by making

use of a variety of instruments which in the course of time amount
to a more or less coherent package. This will often require
discipline and sacrifice for elder and family, as weeks or weekends
have to be given to attending appropriate events. This should be
recognized and allowed for by the congregation.

It is important to recognize that there is a wide range of potential
methods of training. Some elders may find it possible to take three
or six months' leave of absence, probably without pay, from their
work in order to attend a suitable course. Most will have to limit
themselves to summer schools, weekend courses, and day
seminars on relevant subjects. The aim should be, over a period of
years, to fit together a series of subjects which cover the elder's
responsibilities in a comprehensive way.[1]

But the definition of training opportunities should not be
confined to courses and seminars. First, especially at the initial
stages of eldership, there is merit in a system of *'apprenticeship'*
under which a prospective or newly-appointed elder is deliberately
associated with a more experienced elder, so that the latter can take
a special interest in the newcomer's development. This arrangement will be particularly useful where the pupil-master is
competent in pastoral work: the 'apprentice' can accompany the
'master' and observe how the 'master' goes about it. The principle
underlying this method need not become wholly irrelevant as the
pupil gains experience: there is much value in the concept of
spiritual direction, and the lack of those in the role of *pastor
pastorum* (pastoring the pastors) is one of the most important gaps
in Brethren arrangements.

It is always worth considering whether there is a senior Christian
outside the particular fellowship who can be the elder's *confidant*,
with whom matters can be discussed from time to time, particularly
those relating to the elder's personal contribution to congregational
life. This personal support can be of real value at times of personal,
family or congregational stress; and sometimes it may be the task
of the *pastor pastorum* to correct and instruct as well as encourage
the elder concerned—the elder's colleagues may be grateful that this
service is performed by someone from outside the fellowship. Such
a relationship can be an important factor in the continuous
personal development of the individual elder.

Secondly, there are various methods of *self-instruction*. At the
very least, elders need to reflect carefully on their experience of
eldership, in order to learn from their mistakes and to identify how
they might do their work more effectively in future. In addition to
systematic study of scripture, elders need to read widely so as to

expand their understanding of, and stimulate thought about, their duties. Secular education will have given many elders the rudiments and discipline for this process. But some may find it helpful to undertake a suitable correspondence course or pro- gramme of directed reading (a suitably-qualified elder may be able to suggest a list of relevant titles—see also pp. 193–204 below). The elder's reading should not be confined to books. I would contend that every elder should read at least two Christian magazines, both of which should include material on congregational matters and one of which should be from a different denominational tradition —it is vital to the health of the congregation that elders should not become imprisoned within one denominational or spiritual tradition. More generally, elders should inform themselves about develop- ments widely in the church. This implies keeping a close eye on the Christian press; judicious and relevant discussions with people taking pastoral responsibility in other fellowships; and careful observation (preferably by visiting them) of the life and practices of other congregations, especially those of a pace-making kind. These processes may be helped if the congregational leaders of a number of local churches meet together at fairly regular intervals, simply to compare notes about their work and activities.

The environment of preparation

This chapter has focused on the need for, and ways of, learning *from others*. But preparation has been interpreted in a wide sense, and it would be wrong to conclude without a reference to devotional experience of the Lord. There is a tendency in some areas of the Christian church, especially when the first flush of spiritual intensity has passed, for education to become essentially secular in character: the emphasis is exclusively on the cognitive, and on transferring theories and information from the minds of the teachers to those of the taught. Christian education should, however, have a distinctive culture—that of worship and prayer— which should imbue all that is done; here, the medieval tradition contains an important insight. The preparation of the elder should provide for a deepening of experience of the Lord—in this, we should not neglect the essentially charismatic tradition to which the Brethren are heirs. Similarly, elders should not regard them- selves as prepared for their office and tasks without a personal devotional life of the kind which is frequently spoken of, but which is hard to secure in practice. Without such personal study and prayer, our effort and training is likely to prove fruitless. Here, the danger remains that all the time consumed by duties and activities —even training—will eat up the space for this paramount concern.

---

1. Brief details of some relevant events are given on pp. 205–208.

APPENDIX 1 TO PART A

GIFT, MINISTRY AND OFFICE
IN THE NEW TESTAMENT*

Charismatic ministry and official ministry

Scholars from such differing stables as Hans Conzelmann and James Dunn argue strenuously that what is found in the New Testament is church government and ministry in very rapid evolution: that the church in its earliest days was a virtually leaderless (in the conventional sense) charismatic community, taking its guidance from the Holy Spirit through apostles and prophets. Later, within some fifty years of the foundation of the first churches, this God-controlled community had become 'in effect subordinate to office, to ritual, to tradition' in the form of an official, proto-Catholic ministry—elders and deacons. Conzelmann contrasts Paul's emphasis on spiritual gifts and his omission of references to elders and deacons in *1 Corinthians* with the prominence of these offices in the pastoral epistles (which he regards as non-Pauline).[1]

It is of course one of the occupational hazards of the historian to mistake acorns for oak trees, as Whig historians equated the roles of the medieval and Victorian parliaments! Charismatic ministry undoubtedly continued for a number of centuries. At the end of the first century, well after the Pauline corpus was complete, the Syrian churches which produced the *Didache*, though showing signs of incipient sacerdotalism, gave a large role to 'charismatists' and ostensibly the regulations for treating them were designed to

---

*This and the appendix to Part B are modified versions of parts of a study first published in CBRF Journal No. 30, *Leadership in the Churches* (London, CBRF, 1980).

119

prevent them from abusing the hospitality of the congregations they visited rather than to control their influence and authority.[2]

Prophets were recognized in the church into the third century and have, it can be argued, continued to emerge ever since, generally in association with revival, for example, in the guise of Wesley, Whitfield and the like; in the itinerant preachers and teachers which have distinguished Brethrenism in the English-speaking world; and even in the medieval mendicant orders.

If the New Testament is taken as a whole, there can be identified operating in parallel: *first*, a charismatic ministry of the church as a whole, whether universal or local. This derives from the giving of spiritual gifts to individuals on a widespread basis: '. . . there are varieties of gifts . . . varieties of service . . . varieties of working, but it is the same God who inspires them all in every one. To each . . . To one . . . To another' (*1 Corinthians 12:4–11*). The remainder of the chapter emphasises the universality of the giving of these individual gifts (see also *Romans 12:3–13*). *Secondly*, there are apostles (and their delegates), preachers and teachers (as Paul describes himself in *2 Tim. 1:11*). *Thirdly*, there are elders and deacons appointed to exercise authority, and to be responsible for the conduct of the local congregation.

Against this background it is relevant to ask whether apostleship, eldership and deaconship are to be regarded as offices, i.e. recognized positions in the church with particular authority, responsibilities, and accountability to God for performance in those capacities.

Apostles and prophets

Among the different terms relating to leadership in the church 'apostle' presents the greatest difficulty today, though it did not do so in New Testament times. It is difficult to see Paul's consistent application of the term to himself in introducing his epistles as other than a claim to an office exercised towards the church as a whole. But many theologians of great stature such as Calvin and Warfield have argued, as has Brethren theology in general, that the office of apostle was temporary, applying only to the early days of the church. According to their analysis those who held the office of an apostle were the twelve disciples, Matthias who was chosen to replace Judas Iscariot, and Paul 'as one born out of due time'. Their essential qualification for the office was that they had been eye-witnesses (with the exception of the special case of Paul) of Jesus' public life and ministry and, in particular, of the resurrection; and they had been the recipients of his last great commission to carry the gospel out into the world. In consequence of their task of establishing the church, they laid down regulations for its conduct and with the prophets were responsible for determining and testing its doctrine (see *Acts 2:24; 15:22–29; Ephesians 2:20; Galatians 1:18–19; 2:9*). But when the task of establishing the corpus of Christian doctrine and ethics was complete, the need for the role of the apostles as the witnesses to Christ's ministry and resurrection, and the receivers of his commission was superseded, as was the role of the prophet by the second and third century when the canon of scripture was established.

This interpretation remains strongly held today.[3] In recent years, however, there has been an increasing willingness to argue for the continuation of the office of apostle beyond the death of the twelve and of Paul. (Clearly, that of prophet continued at least for a while.) The chief weakness of this position is that it requires the postulation of two grades of apostle: first, the eye-witnesses of Jesus who enjoyed a unique and unrepeatable authority in establishing the church and, secondly, a continuing cadre of apostles whose special role is to act as a 'messenger', 'emissary' or 'delegate'.[4]

There is some scriptural support for this two-tier model. The term 'apostle' in the New Testament is not confined in application to the twelve and Paul. James, the Lord's brother—who was obviously qualified as an eyewitness—is described as an apostle (*Galatians 1:19; 2:9*), and in *1 Corinthians 15:5, 7*, Paul distinguishes the twelve from 'all the apostles' in a passage which is of course referring explicitly to eye-witnesses. But the term is also applied to those who were not, or probably were not, eye-witnesses. It must be uncertain that Barnabas was an eye-witness and still more uncertain that Silas was (*Acts 14:4, 14; 1 Corinthians 9:1–6; 1 Thessalonians 2:6*). The probability is that in *Romans 16:7* 'apostle' is being used in the technical sense to describe Andronicus and Junias, while, in *1 Thessalonians 2:6*, Timothy, who simply could not have been an eye witness, is ranked with Silas as an apostle. Taken with references to Paul's enemies as claiming to be 'apostles of Christ' (*2 Corinthians 11:13*) and the inclusion of apostles in *1 Corinthians 12* in the list of spiritual gifts in a chapter which emphasizes the largesse with which God gives graces to the church, these all suggest that there may have been a continuing place for the office of apostle after the demise of the eye-witnesses.

The role of the apostle was to carry out the great commission to build the church by the proclamation of the message, by teaching and by enjoining Christian practice. It can be argued that it was more than simply the role of an evangelist. It is the role of proclamation, teaching and building up which Paul gives to Timothy, Titus, and Titus's friends (for the last see 2 *Corinthians* 7 and 8, especially 8:16–23—in the last verse they are described as 'messengers (*apostoloi*) of the churches'). Paul himself, perhaps in consequence of his status as a primary apostle, claimed authority over the churches (1 *Corinthians* 10:8) and the right to punish disobedience (2 *Corinthians* 10:6). Following the Council of Jerusalem when it was the apostles and *elders* who made regulations for the church as a whole, it was Paul, Barnabas, Judas Barsabbas and Silas who conveyed them to Antioch (*Acts* 15:22–35) and Paul, Silas and the newly-apprenticed Timothy who enforced them in the infant churches of south Galatia (*Acts* 16:4). Most difficult of all for those who would deny the principle of inter-church authority is the case of Titus who was commissioned by Paul for church building, amendment and regulation in every town of Crete (*Titus* 1:5).

The clearest use of the terms 'apostle' and 'prophet' in the New Testament is as spiritual gifts (1 *Corinthians* 12:28). Silas possessed both for he is described by Paul as an apostle in 1 *Thessalonians* 2:6 while Luke says in *Acts* 15:32 that he was a prophet. But there is, too, running through the Acts and the epistles a definite thread of formal recognition by the churches for work as an apostle. In 2 *Timothy* 1:11 Paul describes himself as appointed. He could have had in mind his commissioning directly by Christ at his conversion (see *Acts* 9:15–18). But he also describes Titus as 'appointed by the churches to travel with us in this gracious work which we are carrying on' (2 *Corinthians* 8:19); and in *Acts* 11:22, 30; 15:22, 40; 13:1–3 the churches at Jerusalem and Antioch can be seen commissioning apostles and prophets for specific or more general tasks of inter-congregational or missionary activity.

The conclusion to which this analysis points is that there is a continuing and important apostolic (in the secondary meaning of the New Testament) and prophetic work to be carried out among the churches. It has a vital missionary element. But it includes, too, the tasks of teaching, encouraging good order and discipline, and carrying out other inter-congregational tasks. Such individuals will not of course exercise a ministry having the same degree of authority as that of the primary apostles. But their ministry ought perhaps to be more formally recognized by the churches than it often is. Ultimately, its influence lies in the humble proclamation of the word in the power of the Holy Spirit and in the churches' recognition of that proclamation for what it is and in their consequent obedience (see 2 *Corinthians 10:1–6*).

Elders and deacons

If the status of apostleship as a continuing element in the official ministry of the church and its continuation beyond the age of the primitive church can be disputed, there is no such problem about elders and deacons. It is their precise roles, and their relationship to each other and to the church at large, which require to be teased out carefully.

In what follows, the argument is that elder and deacon are recognized offices in the local church with responsibility to God for the development of the congregation as a whole and for the spiritual and other needs of individual church members. As such, their ministry is to be distinguished from that of the local congregation as a body, though it is not so much different in kind as in intensity, responsibility, role and, perhaps most important, authority towards the congregation and individual members.

The scriptural foundation for this summary is to be found largely in the practice of Paul and his assistants. That elders and deacons are distinct from the local church at large seems clear from Paul's ascription of the letter to the Philippians 'To all the saints . . . with the bishops and deacons,' and from his definition of the qualities of elders and deacons in 1 *Timothy 3* which assumes a need to be able to distinguish them from other members by a process of selection. 1 *Timothy 3:10* has the unmistakable air of selection for service in a distinct office: 'Let them also be tested first; and then if they prove themselves blameless let them serve as deacons.' The same verse suggests formal recognition, perhaps even after a period of probation, as does the command to Titus to 'appoint bishops' (*Titus 1:5*). The practice of ordination by laying on of hands, though used for all sorts of purposes in the primitive church, signifies at least collective recognition and commissioning for the particular task.

On the method of selection of elders, the only references indicate appointment by apostles or their delegates (see, e.g., *Acts 14:23; Titus 1:5.*) In this apostolic practice, there may be sanction for those occupying the apostolic and prophetic roles described earlier to be more positive in offering advice where they think that it is needed in a particular local church.

Contrary perhaps to common belief, the New Testament does not offer incontrovertible guidance on how and by whom deacons should be selected. That Timothy was instructed on the qualities required of deacons may imply that Paul expected him to appoint them as well as the elders. On the other hand, modern commentators are apparently uncertain that the incident in *Acts 6:1–6* describes the first selection of deacons: the men chosen are not actually described as such, though their task was table-waiting. Nor can it necessarily be assumed that the words 'pick out' in *Acts 6:3* RSV imply a postal ballot! The twelve's words were, however, addressed to 'the body of the disciples' (*v.2*) and their advice 'pleased the whole multitude, and they chose Stephen . . .'—one can well imagine one of those most difficult of processes, among the regenerate as among the unregenerate: a large and perhaps unruly crowd attempting to discover who is both suitable and willing to serve, with those most suitable bound to be looking steadfastly at their boots! It is interesting too that the apostles were content to leave the process of selection to others and subsequently to lay their hands, apparently without further question, on those presented to them when the selection was complete.

As to the *qualities* of elders and deacons, both offices demand high spiritual qualities which explains why Timothy was told not to choose hastily (*1 Timothy 5:22*). The requirements for both offices are in close parallel so that virtually the only differences between the two are that the elder must not be a novice and that, whereas the deacon like the elder must have a sound personal grasp of Christian truth and knowledge of God, the latter must also be 'an apt teacher' (*1 Timothy 3:2*) and 'be able to give instruction in sound doctrine and also to confute those who contradict it' (*Titus 1:9*). Otherwise, they must essentially be humble people who yet command respect in the church, in their public life in their families and in their marital relationship; who are marked by self-discipline in personality, temper, habits, and in the giving and keeping of confidences; and who have rejected materialism and embraced generosity in the use of their personal possessions. If anything, the balance is towards quality of Christian living, though understanding of the faith, knowledge of God, and managerial competence are also mandatory.

The New Testament does not define the *role* and *function* of elders and deacons with the same precision as it defines the qualifications. That may in itself be a pointer: that great flexibility is allowed to determine method of selection, role and function, the content of the job, and the arrangements for operation, according

to the particular and inherently changing circumstances of time
and place. It is possible, however, to detect some aspects of the job
specification from considering the words used to connote the
offices and the background to them.

The connotations of 'elder' and 'bishop'

It is increasingly taken for granted in the church at large, as it has
been by biblical scholars since the nineteenth century, that the
designation 'elder' (*presbuteros*) describes in the New Testament the
same office as the word 'bishop' (*episkopos*, literally 'overseer'). The
locus classicus of the interchangeable use of the two words is their
application to the leaders of the church at Ephesus in *Acts 20:17, 28*.
Both words are in themselves instructive.

Elder

Many societies in different parts of the world and throughout
history have associated the exercise of authority, particularly local
authority, and the administration of justice with experience and
age. They have described those exercising these functions as 'elders'.
Israel and Judah were no exception, either historically or when the
New Testament was written. The use of the word must have had a
clear connotation for Christians of Jewish background or having a
knowledge of Jewish customs. Elders led Israel in captivity in
Egypt (*Exodus 3:16*) and later, seventy elders were gifted by the
Holy Spirit to share the heavy burden of governing and of leading
the people to the land of promise. In this context, it is worth
noticing two things: first, the nature of Moses' burden: 'Did I
conceive all this people? Did I bring them forth, that thou shouldst
say to me, "Carry them in your bosom, as a nurse carries the
sucking child to the land which thou didst swear to give their
fathers?' Where am I to get meat to give all these people? For they
weep before me and say, "Give us meat, that we may eat." ' This
might be regarded as good a summary as any of the elder's task,
and there will be times when the church leader will know exactly
what Moses meant and feel acutely the need for others with
experience to help him! Secondly, for this task of leadership and
government the elders needed the Spirit of the Lord (*Numbers
11:17, 25, 29*): this is only one example of the way in which the
Spirit came upon judges and kings in the Israelite theocracy so that

they could carry out effectively the task of civil government. Further in verse 25 the gift of prophecy accompanies the giving of the Spirit of the Lord for this purpose.

In the Deuteronomic legislation, the elders' task was in municipal government and the cases in which they were required to act were concerned with ensuring the ritual purity of the city where a dead body was found within its boundaries (*Deuteronomy 21:2ff.*); settling domestic and marital disputes in matters of some delicacy demanding a high degree of wisdom and discernment (*Deuteronomy: 22:15, 25:7*); and recovering murderers from cities of asylum (*Deuteronomy 19:12*) while at the same time offering asylum to the man who satisfied them that he had killed unintentionally (*Joshua 20:4*). Later, under the monarchy, elders of Israel emerged as a kind of parliament, accepting the first kings and acting as executives to see that royal instructions were carried out (see, e.g., *1 Kings 21:8*). By the time of Christ, the 'elders of the people' shared with the chief priests power in religious matters and had the power of excommunication (cf., *John 9:34*).

First century Judaism was organized on a congregational pattern, the synagogue; each congregation was governed by a council of elders, presided over by a chairman (ruler—cf. *Mark 5:22, Acts 13:15, 18:8*) whose duties may have rotated among the members. In the synagogue building, they occupied seats facing the congregation and regulated the worship; in addition, they were empowered to discipline members. It would have been natural for the early church to adopt a similar pattern of government (the layout of the earliest church buildings was similar to that of the synagogues) and for them to see at least some of the duties of elders as being on the same lines as those of elders in the synagogues. That elders in the church were expected to rule can be seen from *1 Timothy 5:17*.[5]

Overseer

The word 'overseer' had a wide usage in the classical world, being applied, for example, to magistrates (note the parallel with elders), administrators and even to philosophers when acting as spiritual or moral directors of individuals.[6] But in the New Testament the word is given a distinctive force in the Christian context by its association with the description of the church as the flock of God. In commissioning the elders of Ephesus at Miletus, Paul reminds them that the Holy Spirit has made them guardians or shepherds (*episkopous*) of the flock with a duty to feed it, and protect it particularly from those who would be doctrinal predators upon it (*Acts 20:28–31*). Similarly, in instructing elders, Peter associated the word 'overseeing' with the requirement that they should tend the flock of God and he goes on to speak of Christ as the chief shepherd who will reward them in due course for faithful work of this kind. The language of both Paul and Peter is sharply reminiscent of Christ's description of his role and functions as the good shepherd in *John 10*, and all three were of course mining a deep vein in Old Testament descriptions of effective spiritual leadership which find climaxes in *Psalm 23* and *Ezekiel 34*.

The chief functions of the true spiritual shepherd (pastor) are described by Christ:

(1) Leadership

One of the shepherd's chief responsibilities in the hills of Palestine was to lead the flock so that they would have plenty of good pasture and water in country which was often barren and inhospitable (cf. *Psalms 23:1*). The flock was led over long distances for these purposes, and clearly it required of the shepherd knowledge of the country, of the climate and seasons, and good judgement. He had to know where he was going and prove to be right (in contrast to the Pharisees whom Jesus castigated as blind leaders who did not even know they were blind). (See also *Matthew 15:14*.)

This leadership is, too, one of example (as Peter also emphasized in *1 Peter 5:3*), not of driving as is familiar to us in the west. The shepherd went in front of the sheep who trusted him and followed him. The pastor must therefore show himself in the long run to be worthy of being followed.

(2) Feeding

'. . . he will go in and out and find pasture' (*John 10:9*). Christian pastors have an obligation to ensure that the local church is satisfactorily taught and, in so far as lies in their power, to ensure that the individual Christian can find a rewarding personal experience of God.

(3) Constant protection

By night the shepherd formed the door of the sheepfold; by day he was constantly on the lookout for prey. Both Christ and Paul stress the need to be alert for, to be able to discern, and to neutralize, those who will disrupt the local congregation, particularly through false teaching (*John 10:7–13, Acts 20:29–31*).

These first three are functions performed towards the congregation as a whole. Jesus identified two further functions which related more to the needs of individual members:

(4) Recovery

The shepherd searches for the lost sheep in order to restore it to the flock (*John 10:16*). This gives the Christian pastor special responsibilities towards the backslider, the lone Christian, and those on the fringes of the flock who need better integration into it.

(5) Rehabilitation

The shepherd gives personal attention to the sick, the damaged and the wounded in order fully to rehabilitate them. James includes physical as well as spiritual healing among the duties of the elder (*James 5:14, 15*).

The range of qualities required for biblical oversight of the flock is daunting: the ability to inspire confidence and trust; the ability to steer a statesman-like course for the local church; knowledge and understanding of people, times and circumstances; discernment; wisdom; a loving care and concern for others; the ability to handle people sensitively and to counsel wisely and effectively; sound doctrinal foundations; the ability to instruct; and the ability to dispute with Christ's enemies. Two qualities are however given specific emphasis by Christ: an intimate knowledge of and relationship with the flock as a whole and with individual members (*John 10:3–15*); and self-sacrifice—the willingness of the elder to lay down his life for the sake of the congregation for which he is responsible as pastor.

Deacon

The root meaning of the word deacon (*diakonos*, a servant) is illustrated clearly in the apostles' use of the cognates, as recorded in *Acts 6:1, 2*: 'It is not right that we should give up preaching the word of God to *serve tables*.' It is used freely in the New Testament in a non-technical sense as well as to denote an office in the local church. Thus Paul describes himself as a deacon (RSV: minister) of the gospel (*Colossians 1:23*); the wine waiters at the marriage in Cana are deacons (*John 2:5*); and Martha busied herself with table waiting according to *John 12:2*; and *Luke 10:38*. The notion is of domestic service, the meeting of the practical needs of the household. In *Luke 22:26–27*, the Lord applied this role to himself when he taught his disciples that spiritual leadership required the humble attitude of the domestic servant; and on the same occasion he gave a powerful demonstration of it when he girded himself with a towel and washed his disciples' feet (*John 13:3ff.*, especially *12b–17*).

If the primary task of the New Testament deacon was to see that the practical needs of the fellowship were met, what was the detailed content of this responsibility? The host of practical tasks which are associated with deaconship in some churches today (the maintenance of buildings; preparation of halls; keeping of accounts and counting money; and the management of transport) were of course largely unknown in the first century church because they were unnecessary. Nor does it seem quite to grasp the point to argue on the basis of *Acts 6:1–6* (if this text is relevant) that they had charge of the finances. The important point about *Acts 6:1–6* is not that the seven had charge of the finances, but the reason why they were given charge of them—the object for which the money was used. Here, the purpose for which Jesus and the twelve maintained a common purse with Judas Iscariot as their treasurer may be relevant. On this argument, the primary function of deacons is the giving of practical help, especially of a compassionate, charitable kind both within the household of faith and, by analogy with the twelve in *John 12:4* and *13:29*, among the poor at large. If this view is correct, it was the executive work of the deacons which gave the early church its outstanding and challenging reputation for beneficence both towards its own and the wider world.

There is support for this interpretation in the views of modern commentators about the precise significance of some of the spiritual gifts in *Romans 12* and *1 Corinthians 12*. '. . . "service" in Romans 12:7 is understood by some commentators to refer to deacons, and "he who gives aid" in *Romans 12:8* to refer to the officer in charge of the distribution of money to the poor . . . the "helpers" [in *1 Cor. 12:28*] are understood to be deacons by many modern lexicologists . . .'[7]

Collective responsibility

Christianity was born in a Jewish environment where, whatever

may have been true of the Roman and Greek worlds, government
was organized on oligarchic rather than monarchic lines. The
Sanhedrin comprised 71 members, with the chairmanship undertaken by the high priest. As already noted, the synagogue was
ruled by a council of elders. Whether or not for this reason, group
responsibility was a prominent pattern in the early church. It was
elders whom Paul appointed in every church of south Galatia (*Acts
14:23*) and 'elders in every town' whom Titus was instructed to
appoint (*Titus 1:5*). In *1 Timothy* this eldership is actually described
as a board which acted in concert, Paul being one of them, to
appoint Timothy to his task (*1 Timothy 4:14, 2 Timothy 1:6*). Seven
men of good repute were chosen by the Hellenist disciples to
manage the daily distribution. It was the apostles and elders of the
Jerusalem church to whom the church at Antioch sent a deputation
(Paul, Barnabas 'and some of the others') to deliberate on the
question and it was a deputation which the apostles and elders
sent back to Antioch with their instructions (*Acts 15:2, 22*). Finally,
in the letter to the Galatians where Paul is seeking to stress that his
gospel to the Gentiles was received directly from God by individual
and personal revelation, he is careful to note that his teaching was
tested at Jerusalem by 'them . . . (i.e.) those who were of repute'
and that it was James, Peter and John who commissioned Paul and
Barnabas to take the gospel to the Gentiles (*Galatians 2:2, 9*).

Office and the ministry of the church

There is a strong case to be made that the New Testament takes a
high view of the role of the body as a whole in government as well
as in ministry. The church is composed of members who, while
differing in spiritual maturity, have equality of standing before
God and equality of access to him. All have the indwelling
presence of the Holy Spirit; all are open to divine guidance; and
spiritual gifts are widely given. Moreover, all are enjoined to be
humble, especially those who lead and exercise spiritual gifts.
Leaders are told they are to be the servants of all, just as the Master
was the servant of all. Indeed, there is the example of the Master in
the intimate relationship which he had with his disciples and his
promotion of them from the status of servants to friends (*John
15:13–15*). The general tenor of the early chapters of *The Acts of the
Apostles* is of an intimate association between the apostles,
prophets, elders, and deacons and their congregations in the
affairs of the church. On the immediate question of leadership and

government, there was at least one important instance—no less than the council of Jerusalem—when the decision of the apostles and elders enjoyed the acclaim of 'the whole church' before it was conveyed by letter to Antioch. When it arrived, it was the congregation which heard the letter read, just as it had been the congregation which had dispatched the deputation to Jerusalem in the first place (*Acts 15:3, 22, 30*). The same pattern is followed in the Pauline letters which are normally addressed to whole churches rather than to individuals or just the elders and deacons.

The scriptural model of the relationship between a congregation and their elders and deacons is a familiar one. It is the willing submission of equals to those responsible to God for them: just as the son submits himself to the father; and the wife to her husband; so the church member is required to submit himself willingly to his elders for the common good. The father is of course worthy to be submitted to; the husband must be worthy of his wife's respect; elders must show themselves worthy of the respect of their congregation.

The organic nature of Christian leadership and ministry

The New Testament shows much flexibility in detailed local arrangements for church government and leadership. Nor can precise boundaries be drawn by exegesis between the roles and offices of apostle, prophet, elder, teacher, pastor, and deacon. Apostles and prophets were not confined to an itinerant ministry, as the *Didache* suggested they ought to be:[8] they showed a notable tendency to settle down in one place for a period and to play a prominent role in a local church. And exercise of the gift of prophecy was common in the local church as numerous references in *The Acts* and the epistles show. Nor can sharp lines be drawn between the roles and offices of an official ministry on the one hand, and the ministry of the whole church on the other. Still less is it wise to deny one or the other. Those who try to do so may well fail to catch the true identity of leadership and ministry as depicted in the New Testament.

1. Hans Conzelmann, *History of primitive Christianity* trans. John Steely, (London: Darton, Longman and Todd, 1973) esp. pp. 73 & 74 and J. D. G. Dunn, *Jesus and the Spirit*, (London: SCM Press, 1975) p. 349.

2. *Early Christian Writings: The apostolic fathers,* trans. Maxwell Staniforth (London: Penguin Books, 1968), pp. 227–235, especially 234.

3. Rev. Michael Harper, while accepting the apostolic ministry of the church as a

whole, argues that 'It is best, surely, to see the apostolic office, in the sense of an authoritative ministry in the church, as being intended only for the early days of the church. In the secondary sense, as messengers or missionaries, the ministry has continued. Indeed it is an important aspect of the total ministry of the church . . .' Subsequently he adduces other quite different arguments, essentially practical and managerial, to under-pin the office of Anglican bishop. *Let My People Grow: Ministry and Leadership in the Church* (London: Hodder & Stoughton, 1977) pp. 49–51; 81–83; 184–193; and 198–201.

4. As the Rev. David Watson puts it, '. . . the apostles of today are those who travel as representatives or ambassadors of Christ for the purpose of establishing churches or encouraging Christians in their faith.' *I Believe in the Church* (London: Hodder & Stoughton, 1978) p. 258.

5. For the influence of the synagogue on the practice of the early church, see Ralph Martin, *Worship in the early church* (London: Marshall, Morgan, and Scott, new ed. 1974). See also the articles on 'elder', 'presbyter', and 'synagogue' in *The New Bible Dictionary* (London: Inter-Varsity Press, 1962).

6. See *New Bible Dictionary*, article on 'bishop'.

7. D. Bridges and D. Phypers, *Spiritual gifts and the church* (London: Inter-Varsity Press, 1973) p. 46.

8. *Early Christian Writings*, p. 233.

APPENDIX 2 TO PART A

THE MINISTRY AND LEADERSHIP OF WOMEN

It is not possible to publish a book on ministry and leadership in the local church of the 21st century without making some comment on the part that women can expect to play in these tasks. This does not intend to be a book on the role and ministry of women, and in the last twenty years there have been a number of full-scale treatments of the subject from differing interpretative viewpoints.[1] A short appendix should not attempt to duplicate this work. Accordingly, it does not seek to do more than to sketch out an argument and refer to the sources.

We live in a society which in the last generation has made strenuous efforts to end discrimination against women, in the workplace, in the home, within marriage in respect of property, and in their treatment by significant institutions such as banks, building societies and insurance companies. That trend has presented challenges for Christendom and we are confronted with the stresses being experienced by the Church of England on the question of the ordination of women. This alone has sensitised society in the United Kingdom to the role and status given to women in Christian communities. Those involved in evangelising younger women know from experience what an obstacle beliefs about the church's teaching on the role and status of women can be. It is therefore crucial that churches which are successful in evangelising young women should have clear answers to the questions which they are likely to pose on attitudes towards them. Either they must be convinced to accept a more restricted status and role in the church than the one which they have been brought up to believe is theirs; or they must be given some prospect of changing attitudes and opportunities within their church communities.

133

The issue is of special significance in churches of Brethren background. It is true of course that they are not alone among Evangelical groups in placing strict limits on the ministry of women—there are some Charismatic and Reformed groups which have somewhat comparable positions, and there have been recent influential pleas that leadership in particular is biblically an exclusively male function.[2] But few groups have more rigorously excluded women from ministry and leadership in the local church than the Brethren—at least so far as the home churches were concerned. The average British evangelical is likely to regard the Brethren attitude to women as one of their most characteristic features.[3]

To some extent this can be attributed to historical influences. Brethrenism was born into mid-nineteenth century Victorian Britain, which, in part under the influence of contemporary biblical interpretations, developed a particular ideal of womanhood. That ideal contrasted with the reality of unrelenting toil which was the lot of most rural and urban women of the day. In the Victorian era, middle-class wealth liberated more women than ever from this particular form of slavery. The ideal accordingly became that women should not have to be gainfully employed; their role was to manage the domestic household, bring up children, and engage in charitable works (which became a way in which some middle and upper-class women could in a socially acceptable way give independent expression to their individuality and their desire to engage in useful work outside the home). The cost of this liberation was an enhanced dependence on men as the providers (for the single women who found roles in the household as nurses, tutors, etc, as well as for the married). The idea also filtered down to the more respectable and better-off of the working class, with similar consequences for the role and dependence of women.

To my mind, there is a degree to which the characteristic Brethren interpretation of the biblical role of women did little more than reflect the Victorian ideal of womanhood in the heyday of the movement. More widely, Evangelicalism, which was similarly in its heyday, was similarly influenced.

The danger is of course that we could simply lurch from the 19th century ideal of womanhood to that of the late 20th century—it is in fact exceedingly difficult for Christians to escape from merely reflecting in their theology the characteristic thought of their particular age. But, as ever, the issue for us as Christians is to arrive at a fair and honest interpretation of Scripture and to apply it in our circumstances with integrity.

In my judgement three separate issues need to be disentangled in interpreting Scripture on this issue—status, ministry and leadership.

The biblical status of women

It is important to start with this issue because it is fundamental and conditions attitudes among Christians, both of men towards women, and of women in respect of themselves. The key question is, are women in creation human beings on a par with men; and in both creation and redemption does God envisage that they may have the same kind of relationship with him as can be enjoyed by men?

It is worth noticing that the answer given by the Jewish theologians and religious institutions whom Jesus and the early church addressed was both implicitly and explicitly in the negative. It is a commonplace that women could only advance in the Temple to the court of women, and could not proceed that far while menstruating. In the synagogue women were 'frequently, if not generally'[4] relegated to a separate part of the building and not allowed to take any part in the proceedings. However many women (and slaves and children) were present, there could be no synagogue unless ten free adult men were available. Women could hear the service, but were not normally allowed to participate. While the men came to learn, women came only to hear. At least one rabbi declined to answer a public question from a woman on the grounds that 'there is no wisdom in a woman, except with the distaff'; and the Jerusalem commentary on the incident represents the rabbi as explaining, 'It is better that the words of the Law should be burned than that they should be given to a woman.'[5] As teachers women were confined to the teaching of *their own* children and were not even to be entrusted with the task of teaching others' children. The position was understandable, given that Philo taught 'man is informed by reason, . . . woman by feelings'.[6] Women were also subject from time to time, or even on occasion permanently, to ritual uncleanness which affected their ability to take part in religious activities, and could cause the male to be disqualified as well, simply as a consequence of being touched (cf., *Luke 7:39*). Josephus summed the matter up: 'woman is inferior to the man in every way'.[7] And in about AD150, rabbi Judah ben Elai taught that a man was bound to pray daily, 'Blessed art thou . . . who has not made me a heathen, . . . who hast not made me a woman, . . . who hast not made me a brutish [illiterate] man'.[8]

All this contrasts sharply with the creation account in which man
(male and female) was created in the divine image, and to whom
(male and female) the stewardship of creation was committed
(*Genesis 1:26–30*). It contrasts with the role given to woman in
sharing in the task of creation husbandry (*Genesis 2:18–25*), and her
joint accountability for it—an accountability which itself has
implications for woman's status and responsibility in creation
(*Genesis 3:8, 9, 13*). It contrasts with the Proverbial ideal of the
businesswoman-provider (*Proverbs 31: 10–31*). It contrasts with
Jesus's practice in admitting women to the discipleship band (*Luke
8:1–3*); in allowing them to be rabbinical students (*Luke 10:38–42*:
'one thing is needful. Mary has chosen the good portion which
shall not be taken from her'—when Martha was concerned to
occupy the role traditionally assigned to women); in allowing them
to touch him while ritually unclean (*Luke 7:39* and *8:43–48*); and in
allowing them the most intimate relationship of worship (and
commending their love and adoration as far exceeding that of those
who claimed to be religious) (*Luke 7:36–50; Matthew 26:6–13; Mark
14:3–9* and *John 12:1–8*).[9] It contrasts both with the fact that women
were treated in the early church as having equal religious status
with men (*Acts 1:14* and *12: 12ff;* and *Romans 16 passim*), and the
uncompromising theological statements of the apostle Paul (*Galatians
3:28*). There is also the question of whether in the glorified state there
will be such a thing as gender distinction based on different physical
and hormonal characteristics—though that may be to press Jesus's
remark about there being no marriage and giving in marriage in
heaven too far (*Matthew 22:30*).

We must assert on the basis of Scripture that in the Kingdom of
God women are on a complete par with men—in creation, in sin, and
in redemption. They are as fully and completely human as men. In
consequence, they come to God on the same terms; they have the
possibility of the same character of relationship with him. Whether as
married or as single, there is no need (or possibility) of any priestly
action on their behalf by men—Jesus is their priest. This is not
affected by the fact of biological or biochemical differences, nor by
differing roles in parenthood, nor by any differing characteristic
sensibilities between men and women.

So much of course all biblically-based Christians may readily agree.
But the question must be asked, how far this is allowed to act as the
base from which questions on role, ministry and leadership are
determined? There is a longstanding tendency among Evangelical
Christians to read the material discussed above through the coloured

lens of three short passages in the epistles. The effect is to deprive the overall biblical picture of the status and role of women of its force, so that women are in theory and in practice consigned to the same kind of spiritual inferiority as was experienced by Jewish women of Jesus's day and which he decisively rejected. Far from regarding women as by nature second-class Christians, the more reliable interpretative method is to view the debated passages through the lens of the overall tenor of Scripture as outlined above. Redemption offers women freedom from the particular form of slavery in which they have been placed, as it does from every form of slavery which results from sin.

The ministry of women

In the New Testament the basis of the exercise of ministry (whether that exercised in a formal church office or otherwise) is the possession of the appropriate spiritual gift or gifts. Without the necessary gift, there can be no ministry, and there should be no ministry because it simply cannot be effective. While historically the church has tended to ignore spiritual gift and to confine ministry to either sacramental or preaching tasks, there are many different gifts and in consequence a wide variety of ministries (*1 Corinthians 12*). The New Testament is clear beyond any shadow of doubt (including, as it happens, on the authority of the Old) that the Spirit distributes gifts freely to women as well as men. As Peter announced on the initial granting of the Spirit to the church, the Spirit was poured out on daughters as well as sons, on maidservants as well as menservants (*Acts 2:17–18*).

Nor can it be suggested that there is a class of gift which is more directed towards women, or that there is a class of gifts (those associated with leadership) which were denied to women. It is clear from Scripture that women are expected to exercise leadership at least among women, and so they can be expected to be endowed with the necessary leadership gifts (because they would be incapable of exercising the necessary spiritual leadership unless they were given the requisite spiritual gifts for the purpose). Moreover, the passage from Joel which Peter cited at Pentecost focused on the gift of prophecy as the evidence that the Spirit had been poured out, so that it would be seen that daughters and maidservants would prophesy as well as sons and menservants. The exercise of such gift by women is of course foreshadowed in Old Testament, and a female prophet attended Jesus's own presentation as a child in the Temple and participated orally (*Luke*

2:36–38). Practical exercise of the gift is seen some 35 or more years later in the four daughters of Philip the evangelist. (Incidentally, in the light of *Acts 20:23* and the immediately following verses *Acts 21*, it is a wholly reasonable inference that they prophesied to Paul about what awaited him in Jerusalem. And it is to my mind simply quirky to argue that they prophesied privately in the home of their father, rather than in a meeting of the church: such a distinction was of little or no meaning in the church of the time—see also *Acts 2:46, 4:23 & 31, 12:12,* and *20:7–8.*)

It is evident too that women in the New Testament were blessed with teaching gift: otherwise, it would not have been possible for Paul to exhort older women 'to teach what is good, and so train young women . . .' (*Titus 2:3–4*).[10] This is again evidenced in practice in the person of Priscilla who, with her husband, 'expounded . . . the way of God . . .' (*Acts 18:26*), as it happened in the particular case to a man (Apollos) who at the time was suffering from a problem of defective doctrine in a particular respect. The same Priscilla is described by Paul in *Romans 16:3* as being among his fellow workers in his evangelistic and teaching tasks. It follows that whatever limitation may be being placed by Paul on teaching by women in *1 Timothy 2:12*, it cannot be held to derive from any form of inherent incapacity of women in the teaching role—a point supported by the fact that women have demonstrated themselves throughout the history of the church as possessing that teaching capacity in abundance.

If we are to take the New Testament seriously, it follows that, whatever may be our position on the leadership and eldership of women, in our churches in the 21st century we must be working to release the gifts of women in the service of the church. If we do not, but rather are limiting their use for reasons of custom and practice, our churches will be the poorer for it.

The leadership of women

If women have an equal spiritual standing with men, and some enjoy the necessary gifts which elsewhere in this volume have been particularly associated with leadership (including office) in the church, what limitations if any does scripture place on the exercise of leadership by women? Here, we are faced with two distinct features of the New Testament: first, the practice of Jesus in calling only men among the inner twelve disciples, and the apparent practice of the apostle Paul in appointing only men as elders; and secondly the teaching of Paul on the participation of women in worship, particularly in exercising a teaching ministry, and the apostles' perspective on the relationship between male and female. For some, these two features together seem decisive, and it is true that their apparent clarity requires powerful countervailing argument before it would be wise to accept different constructions.

Argument from the fact that Jesus selected only males to be his inner twelve is based on inference only—the New Testament does not say explicitly that we are to understand from that action that women have no place in the leadership of the church. Certainly, it should be viewed in the context of Jesus's wider teaching and practice before we assert finally that that was the clear implication of his action. In particular, Jesus's selection of the inner twelve must be considered alongside his willingness, already noted, to add Mary of Bethany to his discipleship school, and to include many women among the outer group of disciples.

Nor can arguments from the practice of New Testament church in themselves be decisive. It is clear that apostle Paul adapted his practice widely from time to time and place to place, to take account of both expediency and the sensitivities of those with whom he was dealing—see, for example, his response to the leaders of the Jerusalem church recorded in *Acts 21:7–26*, and his teaching in *Romans 14* and *1 Corinthians 9*. Essentially, this was a matter of cultural adaptation. Moreover, there are no doubt many practices of the New Testament churches which we do not regard as of abiding force as matters of principle—perhaps somewhat mischievously, F. F. Bruce observed that the church in recent times has seemed rather unfussed to put into practice in close detail Paul's teaching on the ministry of widows in *1 Timothy 5* but rather more fussed about his teaching in *1 Timothy 2*![11] The practice of the New Testament church should not be viewed as a detailed blueprint which we are bound to imitate in every particular. It is the principles behind New Testament practice which are of abiding significance for the church.

The question of New Testament teaching brings us however to the disputed passages in *1 Corinthians 11* and *14*, and *1 Timothy 2*. Notwithstanding the need to view them in the context of biblical teaching as a whole, they demand serious consideration, because their essential (as distinct from their incidental) points cannot be set aside as applying simply to the particular cultures to which they were addressed. *1 Corinthians 11:2–16* and *1 Timothy 2:8–15* are anchored in teaching about the structure of creation itself (and in the first case in teaching about the relationship of the Godhead).

We must be careful therefore not to dismiss them as merely culturally-directed and of no continuing relevance to the church. On the other hand, it should be noted that, with the partial exception of *1 Timothy 2:8–15*, they do not, on the surface at least, bear directly on the question of leadership in the church, as distinct from the question of participation in certain collective activities of the fellowship of the church.

In itself, *1 Corinthians 11:2–16* sheds rather little direct light on the question of whether women may exercise leadership roles in the church. This is not the place to expound it in detail. Let it suffice to say that it is concerned with the conditions in which men and women may exercise the ministries of prayer and prophecy (as already noted, important leadership gifts). Much of the incidental detail is not easy for us to follow since it is probably rooted in the cultural conditions of the contemporary Corinth. But the burden of the passage is that, for fundamental reasons concerning the relationships between the sexes and between the sexes and the Lord, when men pray and prophesy they should in their dress and appearance do so manifestly as men (and not as pseudo-women— note *v.14*); and women should do so manifestly as women (and not as pseudo-men—note *v.15*).[12] The reason for this is that God has created them distinct as men and women, and this distinction for the moment remains important (if only for the proper functioning of marriage and the family), even though in Christ there is no difference of status before God and in glory the distinction may become irrelevant.

1 Corinthians 14:33–36 does not obviously bear directly on the issue of leadership either. It needs however to be read alongside the earlier passage in the same letter which assumes that women will pray and prophesy. First, it raises a question of consistency between the two passages. Are we to regard the second passage as superior to the first, and argue that the first must refer to private activities; or are we to read the second passage in the light of the first? Since *1 Corinthians 11* contains no suggestion that it refers only to private action, and in any case the distinction between public and private worship has little meaning in the New Testament, it seems better to interpret *1 Corinthians 14* in the light of it rather than the reverse. Further, in its context the teaching in *1 Corinthians 14* should be read in the light of Paul's principal purpose in the chapter, which is to restrain noisy disorder. Just as prophesiers and tongue-speakers should not create disorder, so women should not do so either (perhaps by debating matters among themselves or calling out questions to the men—who were likely to be sitting in a different part of the gathering). The further possibility is that Paul has principally in mind here the task of testing the prophets to which he refers in the immediately preceding passage (see *v.32*)—in which case the passage would begin to have significance for the question of leadership.[13] Cultural practice may also be significant, in that there is an assumption that it was not the norm for women to be involved in the proceedings (note *vv.33b–34*, and *35b*)—a practice which is understandable in the light of the practice of the contemporary synagogue.

1 Timothy 2:8–15 is still dealing mainly with the exercise of the gift of teaching rather than with women in leadership,[14] though the context is significant—since the apostle goes on immediately to deal with the qualifications of elders and deacons, *inter alia* making clear the paramount importance of the teaching gift among the qualifications of the elder. There are aspects of the cultural context of the passage which bring the meaning into better relief: notably that the letter was addressed to Timothy in *Ephesus*, where the religion and philosophy of the city was dominated by worship of a goddess (see *Acts 19:27*), where Paul had certainly experienced angry and quarrelsome men (*v.8* and *Acts 19:28–41*), where there was the prosperity to support expensive dressing (*v.9*), and where later at least there were gnostic beliefs that all humanity sprang originally from a female (specifically Eve) rather than a male (*cf., v.13*).[15]

Traditionally, the focus of interpretation in Evangelicalism has been on *v.12*. This is questionable as a unique focus, and diverts attention from the revolutionary imperative which Paul asserts in *v.11*, *viz.* that women must learn—contrary to the widespread custom of the time which regarded women as unfit for anything but religious and other ignorance. In this context, *v.14* can be read as suggesting that the deception resulted from lack of instruction and therefore that Paul's strongly-expressed prohibition ('I am permitting no woman to teach . . .' *v.12*) was nevertheless of a temporary character—that is, that once the requisite level of doctrinal knowledge was reached, there was the possibility that it could be lifted. This is of particular interest because later the apostle is clear that the elder should not be a novice in the truth; circumstance, it may be argued, placed virtually all women of his day in that difficulty. Certainly, the apostles should always be interpreted in the light of the Master and Paul's teaching should be seen in the light of the fact that Jesus admitted Mary to his rabbinical school—with the implication that like rabbinical students generally she should eventually take her place as a teacher.[16]

If this analysis is correct, we may legitimately be a good deal more tentative in excluding women from oral ministry and leadership roles than many Christian traditions have customarily been. It does not however permit us to set aside two fundamental aspects of Paul's teaching on the relationships between the sexes, which are evident at many points in his letters and which are shared by the apostle Peter in *1 Peter 3:1–7*. The two themes are deployed in extended form in *1 Corinthians 11:2–16*.

The first is the mutual interdependence of the sexes as a matter of creation ordinance: '. . . in the Lord woman is not independent of man nor man of woman; for as woman was made from man, so man is now born of woman. And all things are from God.' (*vv.11 & 12*). This echoes the interdependence that resonates through *Genesis 2:18–25*. It leads to the inference that just as the physical creation was committed to man and woman in an authoritative rule to the benefit of that creation (*Genesis 1:26–30* and *2:15*), so the new order of creation in Christ is committed to man and woman as a joint responsibility. As such, this teaching challenges contemporary views of the relationships between the sexes which would seek to assert the principle of independence to the point that at least one of the sexes is regarded as unnecessary!

The second theme is less comfortable in the modern context, even to those who have no difficulty with the concept of the mutual interdependence of the sexes. It is the principle of the subordination* of the female to the male, again as a matter of creation ordinance but in this case in an explicitly cosmic context: in *1 Corinthians 11*, Paul elaborates a hierarchy in which the Father is the head of the Son, the Son of the male, and the male of the female.[17] It is the fundamental basis of Paul's teaching about non-veiling of men and the veiling[18] of women in public worship, and leads to Paul's suggestion that in participating in public worship women should be veiled lest attention should be focused on masculine glory rather than on Christ as the image and glory of

---

* In this passage, I have elected after some considerable thought to use the words, 'subordination', 'hierarchy' and 'hierarchical subordination'. There is risk in doing so since these terms are frequently invested with connotations of illegitimacy and abuse of power. I seek to use them without these connotations, in the sense of 'taking a proper place beneath, in a legitimate chain of authority and responsibility', i.e., 'ranking under' in the original sense of 'subordinate'. A salient Biblical example of the concept postulated in *1 Corinthians 11:4* is the words of the centurion to Jesus: 'For I am a man under authority, with soldiers under me . . .' (*Matthew 8:9*). Such subordination is given special content within Christianity by the requirement that those in authority should be the servants of all (*Mark 10:41–45*—*cf. Galatians 5:25–33*).

God, the sole proper object of worship (this is consistent with the call for modest appearance in worship in *1 Timothy 2:9* and more generally in *1 Peter 3:2–5*). It is a hierarchy which in part or whole appears in many places not only in Paul's letters but elsewhere in the New Testament, and which underlies challenging references to 'submission' and 'authority' in, for example, *Ephesians 5:22ff*, *1 Timothy 2:11 & 12*, and *1 Peter 3:1–6*—so it cannot readily be dismissed as an aberration, or as an isolated occurrence whose proper meaning is now lost to us.

The true character of this hierarchical relationship must not be mistaken however. It is not the perverted bullying dominance and fixated dependence which result from sin: '. . . your desire shall be for your husband and he shall rule over you' (*Genesis 3:16b*). As Christians we can assert that Christ died to reverse that and every other curse of sin. The true character of the relationship reaches back beyond the Fall to their joint rule over creation (*Genesis 1:27 & 28*, where dominion is given jointly to '*them*', male and female). Indeed, it reaches back (and forwards) even further, for the ultimate model of the relationship is that between the Father and the Son within the Godhead, in which the Son though equal with the Father submits himself to the Father's authority, and will do so eternally (see *1 Corinthians 15:27 & 28*); '. . . the Son, being of one substance with the Father, is differentiated from him precisely in this, that he renders the obedience of perfect love to the perfectly loving will of the Father.'[19] In postulating a hierarchy of male and female in the new community of the church, Paul is asking for no more than the relationship between the Father and the Son—a relationship of unity which excludes competition, rivalry, dominance and brutality in either direction. It is this model that offers an end to sexual warfare in the new community of faith. Of particular relevance to the immediate discussion, it is clearly a relationship which allowed and allows an enormous measure of freedom for ministry, authoritative action and leadership by the subordinate party—see again *1 Corinthians 15:27 & 28*.[20]

The stress laid by the apostles on this relationship raises a fundamental question for the theme of this book and appendix. We may cordially agree in the light of scripture that women should enjoy much greater scope for ministry including teaching than they have usually been allowed in the church. But does the relationship between men and women in the New Testament prevent them for teaching authoritatively, sitting in judgement on prophecy, and from holding the office of elder, at least when these ministries are exercised towards men? This is a question of great consequence, because it is difficult to conceive of any leadership without the exercise of some kind of authority some of the time (whether it derives from recognition of worth in the leader or from respect for the office of the leader or—the normal case—some combination of the two).[21]

In considering the question, it is worth bearing in mind the arguments adduced elsewhere in this book about the nature of the office of the elder. Many of the functions of eldership do not depend on the exercise of the authority of office—just as much teaching does not entail the determination of truth *ex cathedra*. Moreover, effective discharge of office depends biblically on the possession and exercise of spiritual gifts: if women possess the requisite gifts and if, once trained, there is nothing inherently shaky about their grasp of the truth, it would be strange indeed if the mere fact of gender were to preclude appointment to office. At the same time, we should observe the principle which underlies the relationship between men and women on which the apostles insist in the New Testament. That argues that we should make arrangements which give expression to that principle, while at the same time not in any way precluding women from exercising their spiritual gifts. In the context of a multiple eldership, the conclusion would be women may hold office as elders, but exercise specific authority only in association with the body of elders as a whole.

This surveys suggests that, far from the tendency at some periods in the history of the church, to confine women to a meagre or negligible part in the spiritual and practical task which the Lord committed to the church, the Scriptures intend that they should have a wide ambit for ministry of all kinds including ministries of a leadership character, in an appropriate biblical relationship with men. It is not therefore surprising that this is exactly what we see in practice in the New Testament church.

Leaving aside some salient examples of female leadership in the Old Testament, the association of male and female (in a revolutionary way, as we have seen) in preparation for the work of founding and leading the Christian community is seen in Jesus's own discipleship band. Joint leadership of husband and wife is clearly seen in practice in the early church, in for example the case already cited of Priscilla and Aquila who evidently led the church in their extended Roman household (*Romans 16:5*). In the same chapter, there is the probability of another husband and wife team (Andronicus and Junias) who in this case are described as 'apostles' (*Romans 16:7*). Moreover the normative passages describing the qualities required of elders in the pastoral epistles assume the association of husband and wife in church leadership as a matter of principle. (In this context, it can be noted that if the 'women' of *1 Timothy 3:11* are held not to be women deacons, the reference must be to the wives of both elders and deacons—implying that Paul expected them to be associated with their husbands in ministry and therefore themselves to need qualifications for the task. If, on the other hand, the reference is to women deacons, we have a specific example in which Paul affirms that women may hold office involving authoritative leadership—matching his approval of Phoebe's work in that office (*Romans 16:1–2*).)

On grounds of status, gift, and the teaching and practice of Jesus and the early church, it seems to me hard to question the proposition that women may be involved in church leadership in association with men. Recognition of this principle alone would do much to release the gifts of women for more positive service in evangelical churches.

The discussion of whether women may be church leaders therefore reduces itself to a question as to whether female leadership can be exercised only under the general supervision and authority of associated male leaders, or whether female leadership may also be exercised wholly independently. For the reasons given, it is to be doubted whether that is to be regarded as the biblical norm, any more than the monarchical leadership of a man is to be regarded as the biblical norm—which is not to say that the Lord will not on occasion put his blessing upon both wherever such service is sincerely dedicated to him. In any case, as thus narrowly drawn, the question has something of a theoretical character for those who are committed on the basis of scripture to group or team leadership. For those with that commitment stress the importance of the association of leaders with others, for mutual support, testing and where necessary restraint. Such a framework should have no difficulty in accommodating female members, whether or not the wives of other members of the group, since all operate more under the authority of the group than under their authority as individuals. I believe that the teaching of scripture is that such joint working of men and women, whether or not married, is not only permitted by scripture, but positively encouraged by it as the design of God in creation and still more so in redemption.

---

1. See page 195 below for details of some relevant items.
2. See, e.g., J. David Pawson, *Leadership is male*, Crowborough: Highland, 1988.

3. Curiously, despite the theoretical position of the home churches, Brethren women have been allowed to make an enormous contribution to UK foreign missionary endeavour over the last century, including in what has effectively been church leadership. This may have been because the 'natives' to whom they ministered were thought of as on a par with children, and therefore as permitted objects of women's ministry.

4. James B. Hurley, *Man and woman in biblical perspective: a study in role relationships and authority*, Leicester: Inter-Varsity Press, 1981, p. 61.

5. Rabbi Eliezer ben Azariah, quoted in *ibid.*, p. 62.

6. Quoted in *ibid.*, p. 62.

7. Quoted in *ibid.*, p. 61.

8. Quoted in *ibid.*, p. 62.

9. I have deliberately given prominence to Luke's accounts since he was such a close associate of Paul and what he wrote is therefore of particular relevance to interpreting Paul's teaching.

10. Note the contrast with the rabbinic restriction of women to the teaching of their own children—see p. 135 above.

11. 'Women in the Church: a Biblical Survey' in ed. Arthur Henderson, *Women in the Church, Christian Brethren Review Journal*, No. 33, December 1982, p. 11.

12. It is frankly unclear whether *vv.13–15* mean that the woman praying or prophesying should be veiled, or whether her hair kept in a female style is the necessary veil.

13. So James B. Hurley, *Man and woman in biblical perspective: a study in role relationships and authority*, Leicester: Inter-Varsity Press, 1981, pp. 185–194, in which he concludes: 'the intent of this passage is to teach that women ought not to participate in the examination of the prophets, an exercise which Paul understood as incompatible with the subordinate role which he considered God had assigned to women in the home and in the church. The passage does not in any way stand in opposition to 1 *Corinthians 11*, which specificially presumes that women will speak to pray and prophesy in the church. Nor is it in conflict with the teaching of chapters 12–14, which assume that the various members of the body of Christ will all participate in the corporate meetings.' (p. 193).

14. Something here depends on how the 'or' in verse 12 is to be understood— whether the apostle is citing two things which may not be done, or whether the second clause is additive, indicating specifically what may not be taught. See Richard Clark Kroeger and Catherine Clark Kroeger, *I suffer not a Woman: Rethinking 1 Timothy 2:11–15 in the light of ancient evidence*, Mich.: Baker Book House, 1992, pp. 83–84 and 189–192.

15. Kroeger and Kroeger, *op. cit.*, *passim*, and Martin Scott, *The role and ministry of women*, Esher: Word (UK) and Pioneer, 1992, pp. 78–80.

16. There is also the argument of the Kroegers that a legitimate construction of the verse (indeed in their view the probable one in the light of both linguistic and archaelogical evidence) is on the lines 'I do not permit woman to teach nor to represent herself as originator of man but she is to be in conformity [with the Scriptures] [or that she keeps it a secret.] For Adam was created first, then Eve.' I am not qualified to assess the extensive evidence and argument adduced for this. It certainly makes sense of the immediately following words. But on the other hand the thread of improperly taking to oneself independent decision and responsibility runs through the various possible translations of the key verb (to begin something; to be primarily responsible for a condition or action, especially murder; to rule; to dominate; to usurp power or rights from another; to claim ownership, sovereignty, or authorship). That fits well with the apostle Paul's thought elsewhere about the

relationships between the sexes (see pp. 142–3 below). (See Kroeger, *op. cit.*, pp. 79–104.) In the light of these uncertainties, it should be remembered that it is an important principle of Biblical interpretation not to base a doctrine with important consequences on a text of uncertain meaning.

17. It has been widely argued in recent years that 'head' is to be translated in the sense of 'source' or 'origin' rather than 'authority'. C. K. Barrett and Gordon Fee adopt this view (C. K. Barrett, *A commentary on the first epistle to the Corinthians*, London: Adam and Charles Black, second edition, 1971, pp. 248–9; and Gordon D. Fee, *The First Epistle to the Corinthians*, Grand Rapids, Mich.: Eerdmans, 1978, pp. 501–505). Peter Cotterell, Max Turner and Wayne Grudem have argued strongly in the contrary sense however (Peter Cotterell and Max Turner, *Linguistics and Biblical Interpretation*, London: SPCK, 1989; and Wayne Grudem, 'The meaning of *Kephalē* ('Head'): A response to recent studies' in John Piper and Wayne Grudem (eds), *Recovering Biblical Manhood and Womanhood*, Wheaton, Ill.: Crossway Books, 1991, pp. 425–468). The discussion is conveniently summarised in Martin Scott, *The role and ministry of women*, Esher: Word UK/Pioneer, 1992, pp. 49–60. To my mind, it would not be wise to allow the matter to turn simply on the linguistics of the word; even if *kephalē* is to be translated 'source' in 1 *Corinthians 11:3*, it would be imprudent to interpret the assertion that 'man is the head [source] of the woman' apart from the extensive material in the New Testament on the relationship between the sexes (see, eg, *Galatians 5:23* and 1 *Peter 3:1*, where the relations of rulers and subjects, parent and children, and masters and slaves are seen as being conceptually parallel to the relation between husbands and wives). (See Wayne Grudem, *The First Epistle of Peter: an introduction and commentary*, Leicester: Inter-Varsity Press, 1988, pp. 118–119 & 134–138.)

18. The veil was a covering of the hair hanging down over the upper part of the body, having broadly the same covering effect as long female hair—hence *v.15b*. It was not a covering of the face, as in Islam. (See C. K. Barrett, *A commentary of the first epistle to the Corinthians*, London: Adam and Charles Black, second edition, 1971, p. 249.)

19. C. K. Barrett, *op. cit.*, p. 98.

20. I do not think that this New Testament teaching is to be regarded as applying only to men and women who are married, leaving some other possibilities to the unmarried. The latter part of 1 *Corinthians 7* shows that the apostle Paul did not expect everyone in the church to be married, but nevertheless that he expected men and women to commit themselves jointly to God's work.

21. The question is also significant because it is difficult to confine its import to marriage or to church life, rather than to life generally, given the emphasis on creation ordinance in justification of the teaching.

PART B

Full-time Congregational Ministry

12

PRINCIPLES AND OBJECTIVES

Thus far, in considering the position and tasks of the elder, this volume has asked no questions about whether the elder should have other, possibly secular employment, whether the elder should be 'full-time', and if so, how the elder should then be supported. But when some historian or other comes to record the present course of that small segment of church life which the Brethren movement now represents in Britain, the most significant organizational development which they will have to note is the rapid and decisive move in the more open churches towards those who are normally termed 'full-time workers'. In the home churches, this development represents a decisive break with tradition which has not been made without a good deal of heart-searching in most places, nor without encountering serious problems in some instances.

The development raises many questions which are treated at length elsewhere.[1] But the most important concern the integration of full-time congregational ministries into the traditional pattern of leadership and ministry in churches of Brethren background; the role of such persons; the impact which they have upon eldership as traditionally conceived in those churches; and the relationship between the full-time person and the eldership.

Clarifying assumptions

Most of what follows are reflections which are intended to be of practical assistance where congregations have not formerly called an individual to full-time ministry, for there are real pitfalls for the unwary which are worth avoiding. As such, they may also be of

relevance to other traditions—for example, to 'Charismatic' fellowships which are past the first flush of renewal and where the
calling of people to full-time ministry represents a maturing (in the
ecclesiological, not the emotional or the colloquial sense) of the
congregation; and on the other to fellowships which depend, as
many congregrations of independent church order do, on periods
of full-time ministry interspersed with longish periods of part-time
or 'lay' ministry.

Supporting individuals in full-time congregational ministry
carries real dangers of institutionalizing and professionalizing ministry in the church—the more so since most people from the western
European Protestant tradition inevitably carry with them very
particular notions of the status, role and tasks of the individual
exercising a full-time ministry in the local church. As many
different types of congregation move towards plural leadership
and ministry in the local congregation, some reflections on the
blending of full-time, part-time and, for want of a better word, 'lay'
contributions to that ministry become of vital importance.

Some preliminary comments may be helpful insofar as they
sharpen understanding of the varying assumptions on which
discussion of these matters is often conducted.

The framework of principle is important. Tensions between full-
time and other congregational leaders often reflect problems of
personality, lack of forethought, insensitivity and, on occasion,
incompetence. But frequently there are fundamental differences of
understanding about the nature of Christian ministry and about
the connexions between such matters as status, time spent in the
work of the congregation, and sources of support in that work.

Elsewhere in this volume an effort has been made to catch the
vibrant, multi-faceted, non-institutionalized nature of Christian
ministry as it is depicted in the pages of the New Testament. It may
be argued that one of the central issues facing any congregation in
our day, *whatever the practical form ministry may take in it,* is how to
recapture (usually) or retain the authentic biblical pattern of
ministry. Specifically, the question which elders of churches of
Brethren background are usually conscious of asking is how can a
full-time ministry be introduced without cramping the opportunities
for charismatic ministry and without professionalization. Those
embarked on a full-time ministry may however see things from a
quite different perspective which centres on how they can exercise
a spiritually effective ministry when there seem to be important
constraints imposed by institutional tradition (of whatever kind).
Frequently there is a desire to exercise that ministry quite indepen-

dently of, and apart from the influence of, those who are not in full-time ministry. These questions need, in my judgement, to be considered by reference to a number of points of principle.

First, concern to preserve the biblical character of ministry against professionalization should not lead us to undervalue the position given in scripture to legitimate authority and spiritual leadership when exercised with the humility of true servanthood. It is in the nature of fallen man to abuse power, but it does not follow that therefore all exercise of power is wrong. Any ministry however institutionalized entails the exercise of *accepted* power and authority: its whole purpose is to *do* things for individuals or the congregation as a whole, and the recipients of ministry have to submit themselves to the person who ministers in the sense of being willing to respect and be influenced by that ministry.

Jesus himself recognized the legitimate authority of the Roman procurator (*John 19:11*) and Paul that of the chief priest (*Acts 23: 1–10*). And it seems clear from the apocalyptic writings that in the Jerusalem of God, of which the church is the precursor, authority will be exercised subordinate to God (see, e.g., *Revelation 11:16*; cf., *Matthew 19:28*) though the reign undoubtedly has a shared character (*Revelation 22:5*). Similarly, spiritual leadership, mediated through human agency, is accepted in the New Testament as in the Old: it is difficult to conceive that Jesus did not consciously invest Peter with authority as a leader among the disciples (*Matthew 16: 13–20*). His position seems subsequently to have been recognized by the disciples (*Acts 1:15–26*) and by Barnabas and Paul (Acts 9:27; Galatians 1:18; 2:2, 9–10—see also *Acts 11:1–18* and *5:6, 22*). Paul's own leadership in evangelistic endeavour is undeniable; and his position and authority as an apostle were vehemently defended in *1 and 2 Corinthians*. Followership is of course essential to effective leadership: there must be those who are prepared to recognize the function of the leader. And function (ministry) plus recognition can be regarded as creating positional authority, i.e., office.

Certainly, we must beware of institutionalization and professionalization of function in the church. There is no benefit in recognizing the office of elder or pastor, for example, if they are occupied by those without the necessary spiritual gift for the tasks. But it goes too far to infer that, lest an individual should through gift and opportunity exercise greater power and influence in the congregation than any other individual, he or she should be prevented from exercising gift to that extent, i.e., from doing more for the congregation than others can. That principle would be the frustration of gift.

Where a Spirit-filled ministry is capable of being exercised, surely it should be encouraged and recognized, and the conditions created to enable it to be used to the extent that the Lord prescribes in each particular case. The result may, of course, be that the individual concerned is accorded greater spiritual influence and power than others. Moreover, if pastoral and doctrinal authority is to be exercised, albeit on behalf of the congregation as a whole, the exercise of the requisite spiritual gifts must be acknowledged as authoritative, though there should be considerable latitude from congregation to congregation for variation in the precise pattern of such authority, according to gift and need in the individual congregation.

It must also be remembered that, quite apart from the presence of formal office and professionalization in the form of a full-time maintained ministry, charismatic gift itself is institutionalized wherever it purports to be exercised by those who have neither the gift nor the presence of the Spirit in sufficient measure for the purpose. Brethren, please note: our history amply demonstrates that neither refusal to recognize office nor refusal to support a settled ministry in the home congregations make us proof against the exercise of gift in the letter but not in the Spirit!

The following chapters assume that there is nothing in scripture which prevents an individual who is exercising a resident ministry in a local congregation from being supported by that congregation and/or others. The Appendix to this Part discusses the matter at greater length. Suffice it to say here that it is incontrovertible that the apostles enjoyed the right to be supported by others in their ministry (*1 Corinthians 9:1–12a*) and the Lord appears to have extended that right also to the evangelist (*Matthew 10:9–13*). It is not obvious why that right should be regarded as confined to the ministries of the apostle, the evangelist and the prophet, rather than being available in relation to any ministry in the church. Nor is it obvious why the right to support should be confined to those who are itinerant in their ministry and not available to those who for the time being are stationed in a particular congregation. The apostles themselves were resident in particular congregations for lengthy periods. The twelve remained in Jerusalem during the early years of the church and it is a fair inference that they did not support themselves. Paul was himself resident, for example in Antioch, Corinth and Ephesus for periods (though he did not normally exercise his right to support—see *Acts 20:33–35, 1 Corinthians 9:12b–18*). It appears that his delegate, Timothy, was similarly resident, probably in Ephesus. And *1 Timothy 5:17–18* contains a strong, if not absolutely certain, implication couched as a principle, that certain (teaching) elders could be supported in their ministries. The same chapter implies a duty to support enrolled widows in their ministry (*vv. 5–6*).

That granted, what are the conclusions to be drawn about the implications of financial support for status and position in the congregation? The biblical answer must be, in itself none.

The most obvious case of status divorced from support is the apostle Paul and his practice of refusing to exercise the right of support leads to some observations about the connexions between the means of support, ministry and status in the church. Paul normally sought not to be a charge on the church to which he was ministering, probably for a mixture of reasons of principle (freedom of utterance and compassion) and prudence. Yet his authority and status were in no way impaired *since they derived not from the nature of his support but from his gifts and calling of God*. On the other hand, it is clear that Paul's ministry was for him the priority in his life: at the stage with which we are concerned, his calling was to be an apostle, not to be a tentmaker—the latter task was simply incidental as the means of his support.

The conclusions to be drawn are that *standing and position in the congregation do not derive from whether or not a man or woman is supported in his or her ministry by the local congregation or the church at large, or on whether or not their ministry is full-time or part-time (in one sense, Paul's was part-time). They depend rather on the calling, gifts, ministry and priorities of the individual concerned*. In my judgment it is vitally important that this point be grasped at large in the church if efforts to encourage a widespread exercise of gift in congregations are not ultimately to end in frustration and tears. There is a risk that full-time people will in all circumstances seek to arrogate to themselves a superior role and status *simply* on account of their being full-time and supported. I do not believe this can be justified from scripture. But it follows also that if, for example, elders have other *callings* (whether within the church or outside it) which conflict with their calling to eldership and take prior claim over it, then there must be serious questions about their status in the congregation as against those who regard their ministries in the local congregation as their priority calling. Frequently, full-time supported people will deserve to be accorded prime leadership in a congregation because of their gifts and the priority they give to the work compared with that given by others.

These conclusions are of much relevance in considering the practical problems associated with the role and impact of a full-time worker in a congregation which subscribes to plural leadership in the form of eldership of the kind commonly found in Brethren churches. It is to those practical problems that I now turn.

Priorities in calling a full-time congregational worker

In churches which have not previously called a resident full-time worker (RFTW), the leadership and the congregation may well have to invest much time and emotional energy in deciding to seek such a person. Hard biblical study and discussion may be needed to convince those who are anxious that RFTWs may not be consistent with either scripture or the traditions of the elders. Even those who have no objections of principle may be inclined to think that the need for a RFTW reflects poorly on their own commitment and performance: 'if we were doing the job properly, we would not need a full-time person'. Such a statement is in itself revealing, because it suggests that calling a full-time person is in essence a second-best, rather than the positive will of God and therefore an opportunity to be grasped. There may be something in this (as a matter of fact it has been observed in the United States that older, maturer congregations tend to need more full-time staff than younger, less-mature ones—this may be a function of the general spiritual fervour and commitment of the congregation at large[2]). But such attitudes are in themselves relevant to the issues of the role of a RFTW and his or her impact on the church.

If there have been intellectual and emotional struggles in coming to terms with the need for a RFTW, once the decision has been made, there may be a temptation to relax and think that it is now only a question of finding someone to accept the position. More probably, thought about whether to seek a full-time person and discussion of the possible role of such an individual will be mixed together. There is then a danger that in the melee of discussion the issue of principle will be the focus of attention rather than the more practical questions of role and selection. In either case, neglect of important preliminaries to the task of selection, and of the process of selection itself, may prove to be a recipe for disaster. It is essential that both the elders and the congregation devote adequate time and attention to these matters.

Prayer and guidance

Some may think that the suggestions in this chapter and the next place an excessive emphasis on rational analysis. That is a serious point which deserves a two-fold response. First, the principles suggested are simple, even if couched in the language of modern management. Using different words, they have no doubt often been applied in the history of the church. More important is the point that no congregation can live other than by the grace of divine revelation. In the past simple and unlettered men and learned ones alike have received direction from God as to who should undertake ministry among them and in what ways (cf. *Acts* 13:1–4). In the absence of such leading from the Lord, all the analysis and modern management techniques in the world will lead to nothing, or, worse, to choices which are wrong. The task is to find the right person for the right role. So the first and continuing requirement in selecting a RFTW is for prayer for revelation as to the role and the individual who is God's choice. Without this prayer the effort invested in defining roles and in selection may turn out to be an exercise of the flesh. In prayer, prophetic guidance and utterance of knowledge should be sought for the analytical task to which this chapter now turns.

Considering motives, objectives and needs

In an environment of prayer and dependence on the Lord, the congregation should try to analyse its motives and objectives in seeking a RFTW, and to assess its present circumstances and needs, with the aim of identifying the optimum role for the person being sought. The process of identifying the role has a three-fold aim. First, it should help to prepare the church and the elders for the presence among them of a RFTW. Secondly, it should have the goal of drawing a template or target to assist in the search and selection. Once a fairly precise definition of the role has been drawn up, it will then be possible to ask what kind of person would best be able to fulfil this role—what age, what sex, what personal qualities, and above all what spiritual gifts will the person need to discharge the responsibilities proposed? Thirdly, if the role is properly defined, a number of practical points may become clearer as a basis for discussion with possible candidates: the accommodation, equipment and support services which the congregation can expect to have to provide, and the likely terms of engagement (hours, salary, etc.). The aim should be to draw up a document specifying the proposed role as a basis for advertisement (if that is intended) and discussion with possible candidates. In turn, the document can form the basis of a detailed job specification which, when a choice has been made, should be of help in two ways.

Whether or not the RFTW has recently been a member of the congregation, he or she can reasonably expect to know in detail what is or is not expected by the church. Equally, such a document should be made available to the church: as some may have had questions of principle, or about the merits of the person being called, the congregation should be in no doubt about what the RFTW has been asked to do. The congregation should also be left in no doubt about what is expected of them by way of practical and spiritual support. If there are widespread misconceptions in the congregation or in the minds of key people on these matters, there will be a ready source of misunderstanding, and criticisms are likely to emerge that the RFTW is doing too little, too much, or the wrong things; or that the congregation is failing to meet its obligations to the RFTW either practically or with respect to the role promised to him or her. The result will be unhappiness, mutual suspicion and tension, and insecurity for the RFTW. Such emotions can be self-reinforcing so that a spiral reaction sets in, ending in disaster for the relationship and perhaps, in a very practical way, for the RFTW.

Defining the role

Elders and congregation should not underestimate the difficulty of defining the role in sufficiently clear terms to give the outsider an idea of the tasks which the particular congregation has in mind. Self-discipline is required to produce a satisfactory definition at a sufficiently early stage.

In the Brethren context, the decision to seek a RFTW may reflect not so much of the definite call of God (or of a recognition of natural progression for one individual within the particular congregation), as a rather unspecified feeling that the church is not making the progress which it should do and that those currently undertaking the ministry of the church are not meeting all the evident needs either quantitatively or qualitatively. Added to this may be the sense of guilt about poor performance already noted. Or there may be reservations about whether the very idea of having a congregational worker conforms with the practice of earlier years.

This is an inauspicious basis for innovation. It is likely to generate on the one hand unreasonable expectations of the results which a RFTW might achieve; and on the other conscious or unconscious resistance to his or her work. It is probably much easier for a younger, lively community which has recently come together as a congregation to decide that the time has come for one of its number to set aside full-time for the work of the congregation. Conversely in the mature, second or third generation church, it may be easier for a newcomer to make progress as a RFTW: an insider may be too sensitive to, and therefore hamstrung by, its traditions.

This inauspicious background would in itself be sufficient reason for careful thought about the proposed role. But there are two further considerations. In the absence of careful thought, minds may move quickly to the nearest analogy, that of the pastor or minister in nonconformist churches of other denominations. In my view, that model is dangerously limiting for the needs of local churches in the 21st century—wider concepts of roles for RFTWs are needed, as explained later. Secondly, some of those seeking positions may have very consciously in mind not only that role but the relationships of leadership which are normally found in non-Brethren, nonconformist churches. (It may be that existing courses available in Bible colleges tend to reinforce this view, i.e., that there has been insufficient adaptation of attitude and course content to new views of ministry which are gaining acceptance widely in the churches.[3] Indeed, if the RFTW is to be integrated successfully into Brethren churches at home without losing the best of the traditional view of the nature of ministry in a local congregation, it may be necessary to establish training arrangements in which full-time workers, part-time workers and 'lay' elders can be trained together.)

Of course, it may well be that the immediate need of some churches, if their present decline is to be reversed, is precisely for an individual to discharge the role of the traditional pastor or minister of other nonconformist churches. The requirement for effective leadership, pastoring and teaching may be so great that that is the best way of seeing that they are met. But Brethren churches (and now many other independent congregations) have a very different tradition of ministry and great risks may be run if a congregation and a RFTW slip into a relationship with concepts of role which are at wide variance. If the need is for a traditional nonconformist pastor, everyone in the church should be aware of it and consciously accept it, even if they have difficulty in embracing it emotionally.

But there are many other roles to be discharged in the live and growing congregation. The wide view of ministry traditional in the

Brethren is consistent with a variety of role and combinations of role for the RFTW. It may be that the full time resource can best be applied in a role not traditionally associated with full-time workers in Christian congregations, or at least not traditionally occupied by full-time people when the traditional role of the full-time person is being discharged by part-timers or by people in full-time secular employment.

This last arrangement, and the relationships which it implies, may often be the norm in Brethren churches which are appointing a RFTW for the first time. There are good grounds for believing that it can prove to be a very difficult relationship indeed. Because of common conceptions of the meaning of full-time service in a congregation, it requires considerable maturity on the part of the RFTW and his or her 'lay' masters if the arrangement is to be fruitful—though this kind of relationship is perfectly common in secular circles and seems to provoke few problems there, e.g. in local authorities (traditionally at least), in trade unions, charities and trusts for all sorts of purposes (perhaps it is a case of the children of darkness being wiser after their generation). In Evangelical circles, it may be that the special sense of personal relationship with and commitment to the LORD encourages an individualism and sense of personal worth which make these kinds of team relationships particularly difficult to achieve.

Analysing the need

All this argues for careful prior analysis by the elders, in co-operation with the congregation, of the tasks which might best be discharged by a RFTW. This should be done systematically by the elders, perhaps by arranging that each be asked to identify in writing the area of activity in which full-time assistance is most needed. Such a procedure might also be extended to the congregation—provided that the elders are prepared for some surprises about the congregation's perceptions of their current performance!

In any case, it may be helpful to analyse the congregation in two ways. First, the elders could list the character and quality of the spiritual gifts available in one and another member of the church and assess the manner and effectiveness in which those gifts are at present being used, and in which it might be practicable to use them in the foreseeable future. In effect, this represents the preparation of an inventory of existing gifts and their possible deployment. One aim should be to identify the gifts which are lacking in the congregation, or which, though not actually lacking, cannot for whatever reason be deployed in a sufficient way to meet the needs of the congregation. This step needs careful thought and prayer as it is normally easier to identify what is there than to identify what is missing.

Secondly, in parallel, the elders could consider the ways in which they believe the LORD is calling the church to develop in the next five years. What are the conditions required for such growth? To what extent is that development and growth likely to be constrained by lack of gift, time and commitment of existing members, or by their personal circumstances?

Analysis in these two ways should give the elders three options in defining the role of the RFTW. (1) They may identify areas of gift which are lacking in the congregation and associated tasks which are not being discharged effectively or at all for lack of gift or available gift. Or (2) they may decide that the priority is in the development of some areas of work in which there is ample gift, but where supplementary or substitute gift is needed. Or (3) they may decide that the need lies in some appropriate combination of these approaches. In practice, some combination is the most likely outcome.

The first approach is bound to have attractions for churches with the Brethren tradition of ministry, because it implies that the RFTW will be an *addition* to existing gifts and ministries of the congregation and will enable present members to continue to play a full part in the life of the congregation. But the gaps in a church's ministries may take a very odd shape, and result in an incoherent group of tasks and an imbalanced and unsatisfying job for the RFTW. The 'lay' member may be able to tolerate a strange collection of tasks. The full-time person will probably need a more coherent job.

The second approach will need tactful handling by the elders and a clear-eyed understanding of the probable impact of a RFTW whose remit is to replace or duplicate existing gifts and tasks, especially as the people chiefly affected will be likely to be within the eldership itself. More will be said about this point later. But in the long run this approach may imply that some elders must be prepared to accept a very different leadership role in the church, perhaps even that they should stand down altogether. This possibility needs to be understood and embraced from the start. It has moreover to be recognized that, even if the accent is upon seeking to give the RFTW a role and tasks which are *supplementary* to those already discharged in the congregation, in practice the outcome is virtually bound to entail some replication of existing gifts and tasks.

The process of calling an individual to full-time work in an independent congregation can be fraught with difficulty. At best it is likely to be lengthy. Careful analysis on the lines suggested above will take up precious time. It can be a sound investment. In some cases, the result will be a definition of role which is rather different from that originally proposed. In other cases, it may even be concluded that the resources for the life and growth of the congregation already exist, whether or not a full-time worker is found. Careful review of the gifts and other resources of a congregation can be a valuable procedure in itself.

---

1. See H. H. Rowdon (ed.) *Servants of God* (Exeter: Paternoster/CBRF, 1986).

2. See Lyle E. Schaller, *The Multiple Staff in the Larger Church* (Nashville, Tenn.: Abingdon Press, 1980), pp. 59–61. There is much to be gleaned from this book about the opportunities and problems of deploying full-time workers in local congregations.

3. As evidence of the extent of this change of attitudes, see John Tiller, *A Strategy for the Church's Ministry* (London: CIO Publishing, 1985) especially pp. 115–131.

13

PATTERNS

This chapter attempts to review the possible roles which might currently be undertaken on a full-time basis in a local congregation and to consider some of their implications. It is imperative that the task of defining the role should be undertaken with sufficient breadth of thought, or divinely-intended opportunities may be missed.

Possible roles and tasks

There is in fact a wide variety of roles and tasks which a resident full-time worker might discharge within a congregation. Each has its own implications for the gifts, age, character, personality, and circumstances of the worker. The following summarizes only the main possibilities, with some specific comments. It will be seen that some are obviously closely related to specific spiritual gifts suggested in the New Testament, while others require a wider range of gifts. The roles here described seem to me to be the main possibilities, but the list is not intended as exhaustive.

The first four are tasks which are closely related to each other. Many churches may be inclined to regard them as the chief priority for full-time assistance.

(1)   *Teaching*

Many congregations recognize a need to move away from the

fragmented teaching ministry which has in the past resulted from the practice of sharing teaching widely not only among members of the congregation (often it appears, on the principle of Buggins' turn next) but also from neighbouring churches. Even where a church wishes to concentrate teaching in the hands of fewer gifted individuals among their own number, there is often a lack of people who can give the time to study and preparation which a more systematic and pastoral ministry requires. Moreover, Brethren churches have generally tended to define teaching much too narrowly, as that done from the platform in the full meeting of the congregation. There is however an important and sadly neglected scope for nurturing young Christians and training church members for individual tasks and leadership of specific activities. As this generally requires teaching of small groups and content closely adjusted to the immediate need, it is time consuming and often beyond the resources of elders and others in full-time secular employment.

(2) *Pastoring*

Many churches of Brethren background, and certainly elderships, would feel that there is an even greater need for more systematic, regular, prompt and effective pastoring to meet the varied and complex needs of the average congregation. It is this that an eldership of individuals in full-time employment often recognizes that it is least able to provide.

(3) *Strategic thinking and leadership*

Elderships, especially those in smaller churches, often lack individuals among them with the prophetic, visionary gift to see the way in which the Lord wishes the particular congregation to develop, and the wider experience to know what developments in other churches are proving profitable for life and growth there. This can be critical to the fortunes of a congregation and to that congregation's view of the competence of its eldership. It can sometimes be provided in respect of a number of churches by an itinerant pastor and teacher who is in an apostolic role with respect to those congregations. But in other circumstances, it may be a vital contribution to be made by a RFTW.

(4) *Administration and co-ordination*

In other congregations the central problem may not lie in the area of vision but of *implementation* and *communication*. There may be no shortage of ideas as to what ought to be done to encourage life and growth, and no shortage of plans to put those ideas into effect. But the elders, deacons and others in the church may lack the time and energy to carry them into effect, as well as effectively to discharge all their other tasks. This entails more than simple secretarial or clerical assistance. It may, for example, be decided that the teaching ministry should take such and such a shape, with a blending of contributions from gifted individuals inside the congregation and itinerant preachers as well. But the plan must be communicated promptly and effectively to the people concerned in order to carry it into effect. Or there may be a plan to develop a particular sort of outreach activity requiring the identification, co-ordination and training of a number of individuals with suitable gifts within the church, and the plan lies fallow for want of an individual to invest the time in carrying it into effect. And in addition there is the blending of plans into a coherent whole and their presentation to the congregation as such. (Communication within the congregation is a role in its own right which is not considered in the present listing.)

(5) *Evangelism*

Since one of the prime reasons that churches of Brethren background have turned to RFTWs is to reverse their declining fortunes, many may incline to give priority to the role of evangelist in order to secure a new movement forward of the congregation and growth in numbers through conversion. This may not necessarily be a wise decision where the fundamental problems of the congregation lie in spiritual areas which call, as a precondition of numerical growth, for the gifts and roles already described. But where it is considered that evangelism is the appropriate role for the RFTW, it is worth defining more closely the precise types of evangelistic task which are contemplated; this should help in the identification of an appropriate person. There are at least three functional possibilities, though a particular individual may of course be gifted to work in all three ways:

a. A 'preaching' evangelist

This is a role familiar in Brethren churches in the past. The main task of such an individual would be the direct proclamation of the gospel in meetings specifically convened for that purpose, ranging from meetings of the mission type, to coffee mornings and other house meetings. When this pattern of evangelism is followed, the onus of contact with non-Christians rests very much with individual believers within the congregation. It follows that the evangelist or someone else must be capable of motivating the congregation as a whole towards personal witness and evangelism. Traditionally, such 'preaching' evangelists have maintained an itinerant ministry and it seems doubtful how far a ministry of this type could be concentrated in a single congregation unless either that congregation forms a base for a geographically wider evangelistic ministry for a considerable portion of the year, or the ministry is combined with some other ministry within the congregation, e.g. a pastoral role.

b. Neighbourhood, community evangelist

An individual with suitable gifts and inclinations (which would need to extend well beyond preaching) could well maintain a resident ministry in a congregation if his or her role were to spearhead a programme of pre-evangelistic and evangelistic activity in the neighbourhood. Typically, this might entail analysis of the neighbourhood and its spiritual needs, the devising of plans of action with suitable mechanisms for contact (e.g. house to house visitation, community action, and house meetings for neighbours and other contacts),[1] and the nurturing of converts in groups separate from the main meetings of the church so as to provide the necessary teaching and social bridge into the full fellowship of the church. This is in essence a task of church planting and the RFTW would require the appropriate gifts. Insofar as it is carried out within a single congregation, it could be regarded as a task of replanting the congregation from within (very necessary in the case of some fellowships which, though considerable in numbers, may in effect be moribund evangelistically). In many areas, there may be opportunities for such a RFTW to lead personnel from a live congregation in church planting operations nearby, e.g. on an unchurched estate or in church buildings which are in danger of falling out of use. In essence, this is a task of planting satellite congregations, and may again be combined with, say, a pastoral role within the base congregation.

c. Youth evangelist

A further distinct evangelistic task, which might be especially suitable for a young RFTW with definite evangelistic gifts, would be a remit to spearhead youth evangelism in the congregation, based either on existing youth clubs or new activities created for the purpose.

(6) *Youth pastor or leader*

A congregation which has or could develop extensive youth activities in terms of youth clubs and outreach could consider the appointment of a full-time youth leader or worker. This is specialized and demanding work for which some kind of appropriate training is desirable. To be effective such clubs need to operate on more than one evening a week, and preferably on virtually every evening. Such is the character of this work that it is not reasonable to expect an individual carrying other heavy responsibilities in a congregation to undertake it. Often in the past, youth work has been undertaken by, e.g. a teacher in his or her spare time, and he or she has exhausted himself or herself in the process. It is therefore a suitable role to be undertaken on a full-time basis if growth and development is sought. Where there are a number of teenagers and young adults in a congregation, or where youth activities are successful in bringing young converts into the fellowship of the church, a full-time youth worker can be expected to grow into a position of leadership in respect of younger church members. They will naturally look to him or her for pastoral care and it will be wise to look for leadership and pastoral gifts in a youth worker, as well as evangelistic ambitions and technical competence and training in youth work.

(7) *Community care-social worker*

In modern conditions many people have no natural disposition towards the Christian faith and church attendance. So an essential precursor of effective evangelism is action to establish a congregation's credentials in the neighbourhood. This can take a number of different forms. It may be involvement in the activities of a local secular community centre or in projects for the unemployed. It may be practical advice on the day-to-day problems which people may have with housing, employment and social benefits, counselling. It may be full-scale community care. Some work of this type may well draw on expertise available in the congregation as a whole (e.g. legal, accounting, or local government knowledge). But its effectiveness will be greatly enhanced if it can be led and organised by a full-time person with relevant training and experience.[2] And in the larger congregation the needs of elderly and sick members and others with practical needs may be great enough in themselves to take up much, if not all, the time of a full-time person; in that case, the role would in essence be that of a full-time deacon.

(8)   *Musical director-worship leader*

Some very large congregations (mainly Anglican) have found the burden of directing worship so great that it has proved worthwhile to support someone on a full-time or part-time basis to take charge of and co-ordinate this aspect of congregational life. The musical element may be central, but it embraces other aspects as well. In larger churches (200–300 members or more) in the United States it is common for a 'Director of Music' to be appointed as a supplementary full-time or part-time staff member alongside, e.g. the Director of Christian Education (i.e. the individual responsible for the Sunday School, including adults and training programmes of the church). Indeed, the effectiveness of such churches sometimes seems to lie in the ability of the 'Director of Music' to co-ordinate not so much 'worship' as evangelistic entertainment which is attractive to those who may have had little contact with the church.

Such developments are likely on the one hand to strike fear into the hearts of many people of Brethren background in the U.K. and on the other to suggest how limited are tentative moves towards a single RFTW in our congregations—in this context it is significant that at least some Charismatic fellowships formed in the last 20 years moved quickly towards the support of more than one full-time person for ministry within the home congregation. As a congregation grows, in part through the ministry of the full-time worker, a precondition of further growth, both spiritual and quantitative, may be the addition of further full-time assistance—there is no particular magic in the British tradition of small congregations (though larger ones must be organized so as to provide an effective shared life for individual members).

Three further possible roles for a full-time or part-time supported workers are largely self-explanatory:—plant engineer/caretaker;

secretary/clerical assistant; and treasurer. Where a congregation grows to large numbers, especially if it finds it necessary to acquire substantial buildings and equipment, the pastoral leaders and deacons may well need at least part-time assistance and support to relieve them of day-to-day care for routine matters and to save them from wasting precious time in, for example, doing their own typing. Indeed, on the last point, once a RFTW has been appointed an early step should be to provide part-time secretarial/administrative assistance. (Quite apart from the appointment of a RFTW, many elderships would be assisted if those with secretarial skills were to offer them assistance or, if necessary, their congregations were to fund such assistance.)

Drawing a job specification

A RFTW may well be able to combine more than one of the different roles summarized above. But it is scarcely practicable for one person, however gifted, to combine more than two or three at once and discharge the tasks attaching to the role in a workmanlike manner—by the very nature of things a one-person ministry is bound to be stunted in comparison with the vision of congregational ministries which we can glimpse in the pages of the New Testament. In any case, such a one-person ministry is only likely to occur in the last years of the twentieth century in the West because congregations allow it to happen by neglecting their own contribution to ministry.

The shortcomings of the existing ministries in many congregations considering calling a RFTW may well, however, present problems of choice. The elders may be able to see at least two or three major roles for such a person. Each of the main groups within the congregation may be inclined to press the claims of the role which it for its own reasons considers should be given priority. A moment's reflection, however, leads to the conclusion that it is not desirable to try to advance on all fronts at once. For, as already noted, each of the main roles described above has different requirements in terms of spiritual gifts, personal characteristics, experience, etc. An eldership must select between the various possible roles and search for an individual who is appropriately fitted for the chosen role. Or, if it has an open mind as to the role, it must recognize that it is looking for different types of person for the different roles which it has in mind. Or if it is convinced that, quite apart from the role, it is being directed to call as a RFTW a particular individual, then in discussion with the individual concerned it must define a role that is fitted to the particular configuration of gifts and experience of that individual. If it was to seek to impose on him or her a role for which he or she is not fitted, the results cannot be expected to be beneficial for the congregation.

Once a choice has been made, it is highly desirable that the specific tasks attaching to the proposed role should be listed in detail, i.e. that a job specification should be drawn up. This will be of great assistance to possible candidates in helping them to understand in advance what may be required of them. They must form their own view as to whether the particular post is the Lord's calling for them. And it will help both the person called and the elders to plan the first few months of the individual's service with the congregation and to carry that plan into effect. Anyone carrying out ministry in a local congregation has a right to know what that congregation expects of them, and this is doubly so in the case of someone who is being supported materially by the congregation.

Secondly, a detailed job specification will be helpful to the elders in the search for the RFTW of God's choice. However much time may have been invested in general discussion of the possible role for a RFTW, the perceptions of different elders of the need will be bound to vary. Where there are important variations in perception, discussion with possible candidates and final selection may be fraught with difficulty and the candidates are likely to be confused about the church's wishes and intentions in seeking a RFTW. The agreement of a detailed job specification should go some way to educating the elders as a body as to the detailed role which they have in mind. And it should help the church to understand the role which is in view and begin the important process of educating them as to what they may reasonably expect of the RFTW once he or she is appointed.

Adjusting the job specification

In all this careful thought, elders and congregation must leave room to be surprised by some revelation or word of guidance from God which will lead them in a quite contrary direction to that suggested in earlier discussion. Likewise, a job specification should not be regarded as written on tablets of stone—a natural tendency whenever something is committed to paper, let alone to more durable materials of record! No RFTW can be expected to fit the ideal identikit which has been prepared by a church; almost certainly its initial thoughts would outstretch the capacity of any mortal anyway! Once a prospective RFTW and the elders are confident that he or she is the person of God's choice, the original job specification should be reviewed to fit more precisely the gifts, experience and particular interests of the chosen individual. Moreover, the elders will become fully aware of those matters only as they work alongside the individual concerned. And the RFTW will only become aware of the possibilities of the role and tasks as he or she becomes closely acquainted with the congregation and its life and activities. It would be wise therefore to expect that the job specification will also need some adjustment in the early months of the individual's ministry.

In the longer term, adjustment will be even more necessary. For all its institutions and traditions, a Christian congregation is a dynamic and a loosely-structured community. The RFTW, it is to be hoped, will grow in the course of time. Basic gifts will remain the same but they should themselves develop with further use. Experience, both general and specific, will lead to growing maturity. As in all walks of life, work-rate and competence can be expected to increase, at least for a time. The same should be true of the wide variety of individuals in the congregation as a whole, as a result in part of the influence and impact of the RFTW. In addition, there will be changes of personnel as a result of conversion, movement and death. The particular configuration of gifts, roles and tasks within any local congregation will change more or less rapidly with the passage of time.

For all these reasons the RFTW's role and job specification should be reviewed and if necessary adjusted at regular but not too frequent intervals (a degree of stability will be needed if the RFTW is to realize the potential of the particular specification at any time). At the extreme, the review may lead to the conclusion that the particular RFTW's work is done in that congregation. In most cases, however, where the congregation grows in numbers, spiritual maturity, and the exercise of spiritual gifts, the full-time worker may need to be less involved in the front line of the work in person and, for example, more concerned with encouragement, enabling, training and preparation of church members. With the hoped-for dynamic growth may come the need for the appointment of further full-time or part-time staff workers. In that case, it will be necessary to think carefully not only about the role and job specification of the new RFTW but also about the interactive effects on the role and job specification of the first RFTW.

Such changes should not be allowed to emerge willy-nilly under pressure of events. They should be anticipated and be the subject of careful discussion by the elders and the RFTW in advance with a view to agreed adjustments in the job specification. Where possible, the congregation's view could be sought. Even when this is not possible, the conclusions should be communicated forcefully and clearly to the congregation. Christians tend to be hard task masters of full-time workers and if a RFTW begins to shift role and task before the church is informed, the RFTW and the elders will probably find themselves the target for some stringent criticisms on the lines that the RFTW is failing to do the job which the congregation supported him or her to do.

---

1. See Robert Scott Cook, 'Church Planting', in *Harvester*, Vol. LXIII, No. 2, Feb. 1984, pp. 8–9; and 'Building Bridges for the Gospel', in *Harvester*, Vol. LXIII, No. 3, March 1984, pp. 15–17.
2. See Fran Beckett, 'Serving the Community' in *Harvester*, Vol. LXIII, No. 2, Feb. 1984, pp. 12–13; 'Care and Counsel', in *Harvester*, Vol. LXIII, No. 4, April 1984, pp. 10–11; and *Called to Action*, London: Collins Fount, 1989.

14

IMPACTS

It was argued earlier that what we would call full-time congregational ministry was a common practice in the churches of New Testament times. That it has been the norm in the history of the church, and that congregations have generally derived great benefit from it is beyond dispute. To put the point at its lowest, an arrangement having the sanction of scripture and practice ought to be capable of being adopted with reasonable expectations that it will be beneficial even for congregations of Brethren background. That is, provided that it is applied with due regard for the New Testament's understanding of the nature of Christian ministry and for the present circumstances of congregations—which are very different from those of most other periods of church history, particularly with respect to the ability of most church members to participate positively in the ministry of the congregation.

But observation suggests that Brethren congregations have not always been successful first time in integrating full-time ministry into their congregational life without serious strains and stresses. One important reason for these difficulties is the blithe assumption that full-time ministry can be introduced without giving rise to any significant changes in relationships, traditions and methods. At the risk of appearing negative, the principal purpose of this chapter is to identify some of the main problems which seem to have been encountered, and their causes, and to suggest ways in which they may be overcome. If the result is that some churches are able to avoid these problems and harmoniously to integrate full-time ministry into their life, so much the better since so many congregations are experimenting in this way.

There may too be pointers for churches with a long experience of full-time ministry which are now seeking to introduce into their structure an active plural eldership on New Testament lines (with implications for the traditional role of the pastor or minister).

Impact on the church

The fundamental problem lies in failure to recognise the impact that full-time ministry is bound to have in a congregation and to adapt to it readily.

A congregation may have mixed motives in calling a RFTW. Whatever the case, the whole purpose is to secure some specific and marked impact on the church. But it must also be recognised that in practice it is impossible to realize these hopes without other important but less expected effects.

Some of the roles outlined in the preceding chapter are likely to be more self contained than others. But a Christian congregation is a dynamic and organic entity—a community or society—in which the role and gifts of one member are bound to impinge to a greater or lesser extent on those of the rest of its members. For better or worse, there will be consequences and impacts which are unforeseen even by the most perspicacious members. As always, some members of the congregation will find these unforeseen developments disturbing and unnerving, if not a straight temptation to jealousy for their own position. Such fears in a congregation inevitably create tensions which can focus on the person of the RFTW, who rightly or wrongly may be held responsible for these troubling developments.

It is therefore incumbent on the elders that, in calling a RFTW, they should make sure that in good time they take steps to educate the congregation as to the likely impact of the RFTW, the near certainty of unforeseen consequences, and the danger that the uncertainties engendered by the latter may produce a sense of disenchantment with the individual who is held responsible for them. This disenchantment may seem all the more acute, to the extent that it is preceded by a blissful 'honeymoon' period. The congregation needs to understand that in calling a RFTW, especially one who is in a position of leadership, the need for change in important aspects of congregational life and practice is being accepted—there would normally be little point in introducing a RFTW if changes of one kind or another were not to be expected.

There are likely to be innovations. Old activities, traditions and practices which have outlived their purpose may be altered—to the chagrin of those who may have had a hand in creating them (as, of course, more or less radical changes in their day!). The congregation needs to understand and accept that this is a process which is bound to occur, and is in itself desirable. Especially if the RFTW is from outside the congregation, he or she is bound to bring new ideas and practices, at least some of which could possibly be applied.

In itself there is nothing about this phenomenon which is specially attributable to the presence of a RFTW. Wherever elders wish to see change as a basis of spiritual and numerical growth, they need to invest much time in preparing the group for the consequences. But a RFTW is likely to accelerate the pace of innovation by the simple fact that he or she is able to devote more time and thought to planning and implementing new activities and practices. The degree of impact may inevitably outstrip a congregation's expectations even where there is careful preparation. The situation may be all the more explosive where no preparatory steps have been taken at all.

If the congregation needs to be prepared for the impact of a RFTW generally, members need also to be prepared to appreciate the possible impact on them individually. This will vary between individuals. It is likely to be greatest for those whose gifts and roles are most comparable to those of the RFTW. This will be considered at greater length in a moment in relation to the impact of a RFTW on the elders. The congregation should understand however that to call a RFTW will not generally be to relieve them of burdens which they are having difficulty in bearing. On the contrary, the presence of a RFTW is likely to increase the demands imposed on individual church members. This will be so especially where the RFTW is in a position of congregational leadership and his or her gifts lie in encouraging others to exercise their own gifts and to take responsibility for new ministries and activities. At a more mundane level, as in the case of an addition to the establishment in any firm or institution, the presence of a RFTW can be expected to increase the expenditure of the congregation. This is not only because the RFTW has to be supported but also because the new activities and ministries generated have to be funded! The congregation need to understand that the presence of a RFTW may increase rather than diminish their individual burdens.

For his or her part the RFTW needs to be sensitive to the increased stresses and burdens which his or her presence may impose on the congregation. Tact will be needed both in making it clear to the congregation that their situation is understood; and in forcing the pace of innovation and change. The RFTW will be wise to find out as quickly as possible about congregational traditions and their origins, and in particular who among the existing congregation (or their parents!) had a hand in starting or developing which activities and practices. There may of course be occasions when the congregation are in such bondage to existing practices and traditions that it is essential to confront them boldly with the need for change. Normally, however, an indirect and tactful approach will be more profitable, especially if change and innovation can be achieved within existing forms, customs and nomenclature.

Impact on the elders

Of greater importance for the fortunes of the RFTW and the church will be the impact of his or her presence on the elders, and the way in which that impact is managed and in which the elders respond to it emotionally. This impact and the resulting relationship between the RFTW and the elders can be expected to be all the more significant for the fortunes of the worker and the congregation when the presence of a RFTW is a new and uncharted experience for the congregation. In these circumstances the probability is that the body of elders concerned will have been working together with a tolerable degree of effectiveness for a fairly long period. Each will have developed an established and recognized role within the congregation; and some at least of them will be discharging definite leadership tasks.

The introduction of a RFTW to fulfil virtually any role in the congregation will have a range of consequences for the eldership group. First, arrangements must be made for supervision or liaison on a day to day basis. This can hardly be done with the elders as a whole; one or two must be selected for this purpose, thus affecting their position within the eldership and the dynamics of the group. Secondly, most people who are suitable to be a RFTW can be expected to exercise leadership and initiative within the tasks assigned to them. The tasks concerned are unlikely to have been neglected completely before the RFTW was appointed, and one or more elders will have been taking responsibility for those tasks, if not directly discharging them. The introduction of a RFTW will have a direct impact on those individuals and through them on the dynamics of the elders as a group. These effects will be all the more acute because the RFTW can be expected to devote more time and effort to this work than any 'lay' elder could do, thus magnifying the effects in question.

If these impacts are the case as a matter of general principle, they must be expected to be all the more significant where the RFTW is a person of maturity and experience of life and Christian work, whose gifts and role lie in the areas of teaching, pastoring, strategic thinking, and administration and co-ordination, as defined earlier. For these are the gifts and roles *par excellence* of the elder and it follows that to introduce into a congregation a major new resource for these purposes is bound to have consequences for the elders as individuals and for their functioning as a group. Obviously, the impact will be greatest for those particular elders whose gifts and role most nearly match those of the RFTW.

In these circumstances, a significant impact would be bound to be felt quite apart from the question of relationships, the dynamics of the group and the role of existing elders. For the RFTW has by definition much more of the precious resource of time for the work of the congregation than does the 'lay' elder, and insofar as the 'lay' elders as a group have more time than the RFTW, they have a problem of co-ordinating their action if hour for hour their combined work is to be as effective as that of the RFTW. The latter can give more time to prayer and study; to thinking about the direction in which the congregation should be moving; and to pastoring and teaching. The latter two items will bring closer contact with the congregation than any individual 'lay' elder can hope to achieve and all will tend to bring the RFTW into prominence as a leader of the congregation where he or she has the gifts and personal qualities which favour that development. The result will be a change in the relative positions of the RFTW and the elders as leaders in the eyes of the congregation, in terms of work and role and, more crucially, status.

It is difficult to see how this could fail to happen if the RFTW has gifts and a role similar to those of the elders. If it was the will of God that the congregation should call on a RFTW with these qualities and gifts, the consequences ought properly to be embraced gladly by the congregation including the elders. But it is perfectly possible that none of this will be anticipated or understood by the elders (and possibly by the RFTW). If it is not, it seems bound to be a source of deep tension and distress. The evidence is that more than one relationship between a RFTW and a Brethren congregation has broken down in consequence.

This is a problem which occurs not just in the relationship between a full-time person and 'lay' elders. Similar problems can occur when a new and gifted individual is introduced into a team of full-time workers—associate ministers, for example, tend only to be young and not to stay long in churches where there is an established and dominant senior minister.[1] Ultimately it is a problem in group behaviour and interaction which requires much spiritual character to overcome successfully. Certainly on the part of the elders it often requires a considerable measure of the spirit of John the Baptist when he said of Jesus, 'He must increase but I must decrease' (*John 3:30*).

But in the Brethren (and Charismatic?) situation, the problems can be exacerbated by a more or less sharp divergence between the concept of ministry and leadership held by many elders and those held by some (?many) of those entering full-time Christian service, especially where they have been educated in the existing non-conformist colleges. The elders' concept emphasizes the obligation of each individual, whatever their circumstances, to commit themselves heart and soul in service to the limit of their capacity given their other obligations. Accordingly, it would tend not to accord any special status to full-time work as distinct from part-time or 'lay' work in the church—indeed, it has conceptual difficulty with the term 'full-time' work, since it would wish to emphasize the biblical notion of the full-time calling of every believer to the service of Christ. (My own view is that some confusion and misunderstanding would be avoided if we were to substitute the term 'supported' for 'full-time' in the designation now common). Further, insofar as the Brethren tradition recognizes the idea of leadership, as distinct from gift and work as the duty of the elder, it tends to see it as a vigorously collective rather than an individual function in the church.

The emphasis among RFTWs can however tend to be on the special status of the individual called to full-time service, so that the full-time person is regarded as ordained by God in a sense that the 'lay' person is not; on the need for leadership as a function in the congregation; and on the individual rather than group character of leadership if it is to be effective.

Where there is a marked theological divergence between elders and the RFTWs on these issues, tension between the two seems inevitable, however good relationships may be in personal terms. Whatever a job specification may say, each is likely to have a differing perception of the status and role of the elders on the one hand and the RFTW on the other with respect to each other and the congregation. At the extreme it raises questions such as 'Is the RFTW the equal of the 'lay' elder? Is he their assistant or are they his assistants?' It may be that both elders and RFTWs need to engage in some hard biblical study on the nature of Christian ministry, particularly as it relates to the questions of the time available for a particular ministry, the source of practical support for that ministry, and the significance of the source of support for the position, status and rights of the person concerned.

Managing the impact

It is vital that elders and RFTW together should not sit idly by, observing these various impacts, but doing nothing to assist the congregation as a whole to come to terms with them. It is of the essence of leadership that the leader should be active in managing change. The leader must work on the one hand to neutralize its negative and destructive effects, and on the other to take full advantage of the opportunities which it presents for the benefit of the group for which he is responsible.

If this analysis is correct, a number of more or less practical proposals for avoiding or at least reducing problems can be made.

(1) It is essential that in selecting (i.e. jointly recognizing the call of) any individual for resident full-time work in a congregation, there should be a mutual exploration not only of character, gifts and possible role, but of concepts of the nature of ministry, eldership, and leadership. No doubt, each individual's ideas on these matters will vary in detail from those of the next person. But where there are marked divergences of view on these matters, the scope for tension should not be underestimated because they will inevitably affect the way the RFTW does his or her job, and his or her relationship with and view of the elders. If the prospective RFTW is to have a role in pastoring, teaching, strategy and co-ordination, it will be all the more important to explore these matters. (Elders might of course also usefully ask themselves whether their own views on these subjects are right, and whether those views are or are not having beneficial effects on their own ministry in the congregation!)

(2) In the process of recognizing the RFTW's call, not only should role and tasks be carefully specified, but so should the prospective relationship with the elders and the congregation as a whole. Is the RFTW to be an elder, or a deacon, or what? If not, what access is he or she to have to the elders, and on whose invitation? What freedom of innovation and initiative is the RFTW to have in his or her area of responsibility, and what freedom to

communicate with the church independently on those matters? What matters can he or she decide for himself or herself with or without subsequent report to the elders? In reaching agreement on these questions, it should be recognized that elders, the congregation as a whole, and RFTW will change and develop with the passage of time, and the arrangement should be reviewed and adjusted at regular intervals (without constantly uprooting the plant to see how things are growing!).

(3) If the RFTW's main role is to be in pastoring, teaching, strategy and co-ordination, it is difficult to see how this role can be pursued in the Brethren environment without problems, unless the RFTW is an elder of equal standing with colleagues as elders. If such a RFTW is not an elder, either he will be hamstrung by his, to say the least, ambiguous position, or the position and role of the elders themselves seem likely to be called into question. The implication of this is that a RFTW in such a role *must* have the qualifications and gifts for immediate eldership; this demands maturity and will often rule out those in their early twenties. That in turn has practical implications in terms of, perhaps, abandonment of secular careers, and the need for the congregation to make adequate provision for financial support and accommodation, as such an individual will usually have a spouse and family.

(4) Many congregations feel that the difficulties suggested above may be more likely to be overcome if the RFTW is an existing member of the congregation whom they enable to give more time to the work, by developing his or her existing roles. There may be something in this, but it should be recognized that the difficulties outlined above derive in part precisely from the fact that the individual is enabled to devote more time to his or her ministry than other key people in the congregation are able to do. It may be of significance that an American observer of churches with multiple full-time staff comments that on balance it is less satisfactory to add an existing member of the congregation to such a team than someone from another neighbouring congregation.[2]

(5) It is essential to provide the full-time worker with scope to develop his or her ministry. To put it at its lowest, there is no point in the elders' employing even a dog('s body!) and barking themselves. If God has called an individual to a full-time role in a congregation and that person has significant gifts, it makes little sense to leave those gifts under-employed while the work is done by less gifted individuals; and it certainly makes no sense to limit the RFTW's scope in this way simply in the name of not reducing

the status of another elder or other member of the congregation. This point is of special significance in respect of a teaching ministry because of its high public prominence in the congregation, but it is also relevant apropos high-profile leadership, and the offices of chairman and secretary of the elders. The point extends, too, to more detailed matters of executive action. The elders and congregation need to appoint someone whom they can trust to discharge (and not without authority to go too far outside) the role agreed. They must then set that person free to exercise his or her ministry without constant detailed supervision and reference back to them, except on matters of importance and principle.

(6) This leads to the crucial importance, whether or not the RFTW is an elder, of good and constantly open communications between him or her and the (rest of the) elders. Among other things, this is to minimize the risk of fear and suspicion by the elders of the RFTW. Membership of the elders should in itself greatly help, for there should then be ample opportunity for report, discussion, and the sharing of ideas—in a group leadership, this openness and sharing of important information and intentions is of greater importance than under more managerial arrangements. Where the RFTW is not an elder, the elders should ensure that they give ample time for report and discussion. The younger RFTW, especially, should never be left to feel that no one, least of all the elders of the congregation, is taking a real interest in their work. Attendance at the elders' meeting will be essential from time to time, but contact with the elders should not be confined to that. Elders in general should make sure that they express a regular informal interest in the RFTW and his or her dependants. Whether or not the RFTW is an elder, it will probably be useful if one suitable elder acts as a liaison officer, to be available for consultation and to take a close day-to-day interest in the RFTW and his or her work. In the larger congregation, and especially where there is more than one RFTW, it may be helpful to form an executive group to meet weekly or even more often, comprising the RFTWs and two or three elders, in order to ensure proper co-ordination of work and activities, prompt pastoral action, and to take decisions in day-to-day matters. Such an arrangement can be expected to be of help in alleviating one of the important petty sources of frustration for the RFTW—the length of time it can take corporate leaderships to make even minor decisions.

(7) It is essential that the elders and the congregation should recognize the peculiar pressures which can be experienced by those who have committed themselves to full-time Christian

service. These may be practical: there may be uncertainties about the level of financial support which the congregation will provide, or uncertainties about whether the congregation will be able to meet the financial undertakings which it has made. There may be uncertainties about the future, e.g., about accommodation or how the individual's 'career' in Christian service will develop, or about the need to provide for retirement, even though it may be many years away. More important still, the individual may have difficulties in coming to terms with the powerlessness and statuslessness which are peculiar in a secularized society to the occupation of Christian worker. There may also be anxiety to exercise a successful ministry in the congregation, to demonstrate to them and to other Christian workers that the RFTW's ministry has divine approbation. It would be easy to criticize such sentiments as being unspiritual—as indicating concern to guarantee personal *securitas* (safety) rather than manifesting the *certitudo* (trust in God)[3] which ought to characterize the Christian. To be sure, it is difficult to live by faith (and the full-time worker must do so, even when he or she receives a salary from his or her congregation). The temptation to lack of faith is commonly experienced, even by those who have long been in Christian work. It is not for those who live much more secure and prestigious lives to cast stones. They need rather to ensure that they give proper support to the RFTW (and his or her spouse) in prayer, emotionally, and practically. Above all, they need to recognize that the RFTW, like anyone else, requires pastoral care and support, and they must ensure that he or she gets it, either from within the congregation or from outside it. The informal interest in the RFTW already recommended is crucial in this. For his or her part, the RFTW needs to recognize the peculiar temptations of full-time work and his or her need for pastoral support. In particular they should be willing to receive that support even from members of their own congregation (it is in the nature of Christian fellowship and humility that the Christian worker should be willing to receive pastoral support from those for whom he or she has pastoral responsibility).

(8) Finally, some of the possible difficulties noted in this article may arise precisely because there is only *one* RFTW in a large congregation with an active eldership. Such congregations should, in my opinion, consider whether they should not call *two* or more RFTWs to occupy differing or even similar roles. In any case, for their own good and growth, many larger congregations need to be thinking in terms not of one full-time person but a team, working

alongside other church members. It is possible that where there are multiple full-time workers, the dynamics of the relationship of the RFTW with the (other) elders and the rest of the congregation will be different and more positive than where there is only one full-time person in this, for Brethren congregations, difficult and unaccustomed position.

---

1. See Lyle E. Schaller, *The Multiple Staff and the Larger Church* (Nashville, Tenn.: Abingdon Press) p. 122ff.

2. *Ibid.* pp. 64–67.

3. The categories are, I believe, Luther's—not the least of his deep insights into the meaning of scripture. Cf. *Matthew 6:31*, which does not only apply to missionaries and itinerant preachers.

15

CONCLUSION

The purpose of discussing the integration of full-time ministries into congregations where there is a strong tradition of every-member ministry has been to warn of possible pitfalls and to suggest possible ways of avoiding them. But I do not intend to discourage congregations from calling individuals to undertake full-time work with them. In the larger congregation, it is almost certainly a condition of further spiritual and numerical growth that there should be not just one, but a number of people working full-time. And there would be something strange if individuals were to be prevented *as a matter of principle* from devoting themselves wholly to the Lord's work in the congregational situation, but not in a multitude of other circumstances. Moreover, frequently it will be that in such congregations a full-time person will be the effective leader of the leadership group (though, as has been emphasized, whether that is so should depend on the relative gifts of each of the leaders concerned, not on whether or not one of them receives financial support for his or her work in the congregation).

It is worth remembering that there is nothing special to the church about the difficulties which have been described. We live in an age in which the professionalization of service and care has become commonplace for the best of motives. But the almost universally-found corollaries are, on the one hand, withdrawal from charitable concern on the part of many ('I need not be concerned because others are paid to deal with the problem') and, on the other, the sense of powerlessness and irresponsibility felt by the clients of the professionals. This has led to widespread efforts to encourage people to take responsibility for their own situations and to work together to improve their environment and quality of life. Often that cannot be achieved without full-time help, at least initially. Yet the problem is often to prevent the full-time person and his or her clients from being content with a relationship which perpetuates the essential dependency of the latter.

I was interested by a conversation a few years ago with someone with whom I had worked a few years before to establish a secular community centre. She recounted that over the years the problem had been to find full-time staff who were willing to respect and encourage the contribution of 'lay' volunteers, and, more important, who were prepared to work under the authority and direction of a 'lay' committee. Equally, there had been a problem to prevent the 'lay' volunteers from withdrawing from the work immediately a full-time professional came onto the scene. This illustrates that the problems with which many Christian congregations are wrestling today are no more than a reflection of those which sinful humanity often experiences when it tries to work together. Distortions of relationship, for example, abuse of power and unhealthy dependency on others, are among the consequences of the Fall. But unless the Christian claim is false, these problems must be overcome in the church, where we are supposed to be sanctified by the Holy Spirit and empowered to live out the ethics of the new kingdom which the Lord is bringing into being.

I have sought in the preceding chapters to offer some advice to help full-time workers, 'lay' elders and congregations to break out of habits of thought and relationship which have been common in the church for 1500 years, and begin to work together in partnership in the manner which I believe is outlined in the New Testament.

There are many congregations in the Brethren tradition which are demonstrating the value and opportunities of setting aside one or more persons for full-time ministry in the local church. To that end I have suggested points which elders and full-time workers need to bear in mind in order to increase the prospect that the benefits hoped for will be achieved in practice, rather than being frittered away in uncertainty about role and in unnecessary tensions by which Satan is always anxious to frustrate the building of the kingdom.

Much, I believe, depends upon whether 'lay' elders will take seriously the suggestions made in Part A of the volume. Quite apart from the question of appointing full-time congregational workers, it is imperative for the health of the local church that the spiritual quality and practical competence of elders should be improved and sustained. Where they are not, continued spiritual decline seems inevitable, and it will not be in the least surprising to find that full-time workers become frustrated as they find themselves confronted with incompetence, idleness, and lack of vision, insight and spirituality on the part of those who claim to supervise the full-time worker as well as to lead the church. By contrast, where the life, service and spiritual depth of the 'lay' eldership command respect from the congregation at large, full-time workers are likely to experience no difficulty in working with, and indeed under the authority of, such people. Where there is true Christian maturity among 'lay' elders and full-time workers alike, there will usually be no difficulty about assigning roles to each according to spiritual gifts and priorities, without considering the precise status of the individual concerned.

To achieve an effective full-time ministry without impairing plural leadership and the exercise of charismatic gift would be at once a boon to the congregations concerned and an example to the church at large.

From CEN. September 24, 1993 No. 5174.

APPENDIX TO PART B

NEW TESTAMENT PRACTICE
IN SUPPORTING CHRISTIAN WORKERS

There is no ambiguity in the New Testament that apostles and apostolic delegates were on occasion supported financially by the churches. In fact, Brethren teaching may have tended to place excessive stress on the point that in at least three infant churches, and possibly therefore as a matter of normal practice, Paul and his companions supported themselves by tent-making—they worked 'night and day' . . . not to be a burden to any of you' (*Acts 18:3; Acts 20:33–34; 1 Corinthians 9; 2 Corinthians 11:7–11; 2 Corinthians 12:14–18; and Thessalonians 3:7–8*). But this arrangment should not be taken as an immutable norm. *1 Corinthians 9:6, 15–18* may be taken as suggesting that it was normal for Paul and Barnabas to support themselves; but *2 Corinthians 12:13* may, on the other hand, be implying that Paul's support of himself in Corinth was exceptional. Moreover, his main reasons for declining such help had nothing to do with the principle of accepting support. In Thessalonica, he wanted to encourage the believers to work rather than be idle while awaiting the Coming. In Corinth, he wanted a freehold to preach an unadulterated gospel and to avoid being equated with the false prophets (*1 Corinthians 16–18; 2 Corinthians 11:12–15; 12:11–13*). At Ephesus, his reason was to put himself in a position to help the poor (*Acts 20:35*).

In any case, *1 Corinthians 9* is categoric that apostles have a complete right to financial support and that the churches have an obligation to maintain them. *1 Corinthians 9:5–6* implies that all the other apostles were given and accepted such support. For his part, Paul stresses that he was waiving his right to support from both the Thessalonians and the Corinthians: 'It was not because we have not that right, but to give you in our conduct an example of imitate' (2 Thessalonians 3:9). The point is expanded in 1 Corinthians 9:1–18.

Paul sometimes exercised the right. Paradoxically he did so in both Thessalonica and Corinth by accepting help from the Philippian and Macedonian churches respectively (Philippians 4:16, 2 Corinthians 11:9). The Philippians continued to support him while he was a prisoner in Rome (Philippians 1:5; 4:14–20).

Much less certain conclusions can be drawn from the New Testament about whether it was the practice of the churches to maintain elders in a pastoral ministry in individual churches. There is no positive support for it; but nor is there any prohibition. Lack of guidance on the subject is not surprising: the book of Acts and most of the epistles were written only a comparatively short time after the founding of the churches to which they refer. They were written by apostles or their companions to infant churches or to apostolic delegates. There are however one or two clues. 1 Timothy 5:17–18 refers to the reward which should be given to elders who rule well, especially those who labour in teaching and preaching: the payment should be 'double honour', which is the 'grain' and 'wage' of the Old Testament scriptures quoted in verse 18. It is interesting that the first of these quotations is used by Paul in 1 Corinthians 9:9 in support of the apostles' incontestable right to be maintained by the churches. Secondly, the enrolled widow was certainly supported by the churches (1 Timothy 5:3–16); this assistance was partly a pension for help already given. Thirdly, within a generation or so the Syrian churches were supporting a resident ministry: 'A genuine charismatist, however, who wishes to make his home with you has a right to a livelihood. (Similarly, a genuine teacher is as much entitled to his keep as a manual labourer.)' In referring to elders and deacons, the manual instructed the churches not to choose men eager for money, a point which may be significant because elsewhere the concern is that even a genuine charismatist should not become a burden on the church by staying more than a day or two in it.[1]

There is a further question to be answered, however: how far is it justified to draw a rigid distinction between apostles and their delegates on the one hand and elders with a settled ministry in a local church, on the other? The traditional Brethren position, more honoured in the breach than in the observance, is that missionaries and full-time preachers should be strictly itinerant, so that the growth of an indigenous eldership should not be stunted. But this tends to dismiss the evidence that Paul spent three years in

Ephesus and eighteen months, plus additional periods, at Corinth; and that when he himself was absent, he was careful to send his various assistants to continue the task of church-building as well as evangelism (see *2 Corinthians 7–13 passim; Philippians 2:19–29, Colossians 4:12–13*, and *1 and 2 Timothy* and *Titus*). Titus' responsibilities were towards the local churches of Crete as a whole. Timothy's charge was however specifically towards the church in Ephesus (*1 Timothy 1:3*) and his instructions suggest a settled pastoral and teaching ministry which both he and Paul regarded as his prime responsibility at that time. That ministry, like Titus', aimed at building up the church and ensuring good order and practice rather than a wholly evangelistic ministry. Experience suggests that to be effective such a ministry requires time, attention and continuity, requirements which in themselves seem to make inroads into the principle of itinerary. A change in the character and requirements of ministry as local churches matured seems plausible and it is interesting that history associates the apostle John with one church in his old age and that in later years both he and Peter describe themselves as elders, though perhaps not in the technical sense.

But the New Testament recognizes, too, that a danger of giving financial support to Christian workers is that the system will attract the idle whose motive is to take advantage of those who support them. Paul warned against this danger explicitly in *2 Timothy 3:1–9* and elsewhere he suggests that the motive of false apostles and prophets can be personal gain. The early patristic writings indicate that this soon became a considerable problem in the church. It has continued to afflict it at a number of stages in history.

---

1. *Early Christian Writings: The apostolic fathers* trans. Maxwell Stanforth (London: Penguin Books, 1968), p. 234.

FURTHER READING

The aim of this book has been no more than to sketch the outlines of the responsibilities of the congregational elder. The hope is that it has excited elders and prospective elders to deeper reflection on their calling. Chapter 11 discussed ways in which they might prepare and develop themselves for their ministry. Much of that preparation and development will necessarily take place in their private devotions, and in reading and thought over the years. It is desirable that that reading should be undertaken with discipline and some system, so that the relevant subject matters are gradually covered.

In our day, there is a plethora of possible study material, and more is being added all the time. It is important to keep in touch with the reviews to spot valuable additions to the literature. The following suggestions deliberately concentrate on only a few aspects of the elder's work, in the belief that in many congregations it is these matters which need to be given urgent priority to improve elders' performance. The list is not comprehensive. The focus is on recently-published books (without any implication that there are not earlier volumes which can usefully be studied, provided that suitable transpositions are made in applying their advice in modern circumstances). If elders have not previously attempted any systematic self-instruction, they should start somewhere soon, and these suggestions will probably serve as well as any others.

A. ELDERS, DEACONS AND PLURAL LEADERSHIP

Arthur Henderson (ed.), *Leadership in the Churches* (Christian Brethren Research Journal No. 30: London: CBRF, 1980§). Considers leadership in the churches, specifically against the background of Brethren congregations late in the 1970s.

Alexander Strauch, *Biblical Eldership: An urgent call to restore biblical church leadership* (Litteton, Col.: Lewis and Roth, 2nd edition, 1988). An excellent study, which parallels the subject matter of this book, in a consecutive expositional manner from a slightly more conservative perspective.‡

Alexander Strauch, *A study guide to biblical eldership* (Littleton, Col.: Lewis and Roth, 1987).‡

Alexander Strauch, *They keep watch over your souls: eight sermons on biblical eldership* (4 tapes), (Littleton, Col.: Lewis and Roth, n.d.).‡

Alexander Strauch, *The New Testament deacon: the church's minister of mercy*, (Littleton, Colorado: Lewis and Roth, 1992 (and related *Study Guide* (ditto, 1992)) Encourages deacons to move from a building-maintenance mentality into a people-serving mentality. A good place to start on a neglected subject, but somewhat cautious and restricted in its conclusions.

Lyle E. Schaller, *The Multiple Staff and the Larger Church* (Nashville, Tenn.: Abingdon Press, 1980). Very perceptive in commenting on interactive relationships and tensions which can arise within teams of full-time workers; many points can be tranposed to any situation of group leadership and ministry. (Simply one of Schaller's many works on church leadership and administration.)

H. H. Rowdon (ed), *Servants of God, Christian Brethren Research Journal* No. 37, (Exeter: Paternoster Press, 1986). Theological, strategic and practical papers on the use of full-time workers in Brethren churches.

A. Kuen, *Ministères dans l'église* (St. Legier: Editions Emmaüs, 1983). A comprehensive applied biblical analysis of the varieties of Christian ministries in the church from the Christian Brethren tradition. See also *Dons pour le service*, by the same author and publisher, 1982.

Bruce Stabbert, *The Team Concept: Paul's Church Leadership Patterns or Ours?* (Tacoma, Wash.: Hegg Bros, 1982). Another thorough biblical analysis, from the Baptist tradition, of plural leadership and ministry in the church.

John Tiller, *A Strategy for the Church's Ministry* (London: CIO Publishing, 1983). An Anglican analysis pointing towards shared congregational ministry.

John Tiller with Mark Birchall, *The Gospel Community and its Leadership* (Basingstoke: Marshall Pickering, 1987).

David Watson, *I believe in the Church* (London: Hodder and Stoughton, 1978).

Michael Harper, *Let My People grow: Ministry and Leadership in the Church* (London: Hodder and Stoughton, 1977). Two analyses of plural ministry from the Anglican 'Charismatic' tradition.

Howard Belben (ed.), *Ministry in the Local Church* (London: Epworth, 1986). Essays from the evangelical Methodist tradition.

Paul M. Miller, *Leading the Family of God* (Scottdale, Pa: Herald Press, 1981).† A Mennonite study of congregational leadership.

B. THE MINISTRY OF WOMEN

James B. Hurley, *Man and Woman in Biblical Perspective: a study in role relationships and authority*, (Leicester: Inter-Varsity Press, 1981). A detailed careful biblical and historical analysis of its subject.

J. David Pawson, *Leadership is Male*, (Crowborough: Highland, 1988). A strong plea to retain leadership as a male function in thie church.

John Piper and Wayne Grudem (eds), *Recovering Biblical Manhood and Womanhood: a response to Evangelical Feminism*, (Wheaton, Ill.: Crossway Books, 1991). A very detailed symposium which argues that some governing and teaching roles in the church should be restricted to men.

Martin Scott, *The role and ministry of women*, (Milton Keynes: Word (UK)/ Pioneer, 1992). Clear and concise Biblical argument that women should be free to minister in any way that God calls them to.

Olive Rogers, Sally Hogg *et al.*, *Does God expect less of women*, (London: Partnership Publications, [1993]). Six Bible studies focusing on the biblical status of women.

Richard Clark Kroeger and Catherine Clark Kroeger, *I suffer not a woman: Rethinking 1 Timothy 2:11–15 in light of ancient evidence*, Grand Rapids, Mich.: Baker Book House, 1992. Brings archaeological and historical evidence, and linguistic material, to argue that the traditional translation is not justified.

Elaine Storkey, *What's right with feminism* (London: SPCK, 1985). Required reading for those who attack Christians as feminists without really knowing what feminism is.

Mary Evans, *Woman in the Bible* (Exeter: Paternoster, 1983). A thorough biblical survey.

C. PASTORING

R. E. O. White, *A Guide to Pastoral Care: A practical primer of pastoral theology* (Basingstoke: Pickering and Inglis, 1976). The essential primer on pastoral care. It is comprehensive, and deals with the practice of pastoring as well as with the range of problems likely to be encountered at the various stages of the Christian's life.

Gary Collins, *Christian Counselling: A comprehensive guide* (Waco, Texas: Word Books, 2nd edition, 1988). A non-technical introduction.

Harold H. Rowdon (ed.), *The Caring Church*, Christian Brethren Review Journal No. 35, Christian Brethren Research Fellowship (obtainable from The Paternoster Press Ltd, Carlisle). A collection of essays which refer both to the practice and theology of pastoral care.

Derek Prime, *Pastors and Teachers* (Highland: 1989). A simple but comprehensive treatment of the work of a pastor/teacher.

Derek and Nancy Copley, *Building with Bananas: People problems in the local church* (Exeter: The Paternoster Press, 1978). An amusing and perceptive treatment of its subject.

Ruth Fowke, *Beginning Pastoral Counselling* (Bramcote, Notts.: Grove Books, 1985).

Ruth Fowke, *Growing through Crises* (Basingstoke: Marshall Pickering 1985). Deals with life crises, situational crises such as bereavement illness and death, and responses to crises, such as depression.

Richard Inwood, *Biblical Perspectives on Counselling* (Bramcote: Notts Grove Books, 1980).

Derek Tidball, *Skilful Shepherds: an Introduction to Pastoral Theology* (Leicester: IVP, 1986).

David Augsburger, *Caring Enough to Confront* (Scottdale Pa: Herald Press 1973).†

——, *Caring Enough to Forgive* (Scottdale Pa: Herald Press, 1981).†

——, *Caring Enough to Hear and be Heard* (Scottdale Pa: Herald Press 1982).†

Joyce Huggett, *Listening to People* (London: Hodder and Stoughton, 1988 Immensely readable—and challenging.

Roger Hurding, *The Bible and Counselling*, (London: Hodder and Stoughton 1992).

Margaret Ellis, *Caring for new Christians*, (Milton Keynes: Nelson Word Ltd 1993).

Joanna and Alister McGrath, *The Dilemma of Self-Esteem* (Wheaton, Ill Crossway Books, 1992).

E. R. Stutzman, *Welcome! A Biblical and practical guide to receiving new members* (Scottsdale, Penn.: Herald, 1990)†.

Books which focus on techniques of counselling from a Christian viewpoint are:

Myra Chave-Jones, *The Gift of Helping* (Leicester: Inter-Varsity Press, 1982

Roger Hurding, *Restoring the Image: an Introduction to Christian Counselling* (Exeter: The Paternoster Press, 1980.)

Roger Hurding, *Roots and Shoots: A Guide to Counselling and Psychotherapy* (London: Hodder and Stoughton, 1985). A survey and critique secular psychological theories from the biblical viewpoint.

Evelyn Peterson, *Who Cares? A Handbook of Christian Counselling* (Exeter The Paternoster Press, 1980).

Paul M. Miller, *Peer Counselling in the Church* (Scottdale Pa: Herald Press 1978).†

Peter Ledger, *Counselling and the Holy Spirit* (Marshall Pickering, 1989). down-to-earth treatment from a 'charismatic' perspective.

Michael Jacobs, *Still Small Voice: An Introduction to Pastoral Counselling* (London: SPCK, 1982).

——, *Swift to Hear: Facilitating Skills in Listening and Responding*, (London SPCK, 1985).

Books on particular areas of pastoral work are:-

MARRIAGE, DIVORCE AND SEXUAL MATTERS

David and Joyce Ames, *Looking up the Aisle?* (Kingsway, 1989). A couples guide to friendship, romance and marriage.

Peter Chambers, *Made in Heaven?* (SPCK, 1988). Ministry to those intending marriage.

Howard Eyrich, *Three to get ready* (Baker, 1978).

John White, *Eros defiled: the Christian and Sexual Guilt* (Leicester: IVP, 1978).

Selwyn Hughes, *Marriage as God intended* (Eastbourne: Kingsway Publications, 1983).

David Phypers, *Christian Marriage in Crisis* (London: Marc Europe, 1985).

David Atkinson, *To Have and to Hold* (London: Collins, 1979).

Margaret Evening, *Who Walk Alone* (London: Hodder and Stoughton, 1974).

John Williams, *For Every Cause?* (Exeter/Neptune, New Jersey: The Paternoster Press/Loizeaux Brothers, 1981).

Andrew Cornes, *Divorce and Remarriage: Biblical principles and pastoral practice*, (London: Hodder and Stoughton, 1993). A detailed and rigorous examination—indispensable even if you disagree with it!

HOMOSEXUALITY

Martin Hallett, *I am learning to love* (Basingstoke: Marshall Pickering).

Andrew Comiskey, *Pursuing sexual wholeness*, (Eastbourne: Monarch, 1990). Advice for those ministering to homosexuals.

AIDS

Patrick Dixon, *The Truth about Aids* (Eastbourne: Kingsway, 1987).

Gavin Reid, *Beyond Aids* (Eastbourne: Kingsway, 1987).

PARENTING AND YOUNG PEOPLE

John White, *Parents in Pain* (Leicester: IVP, 1979).

Lance Pierson, *The Pastoral Care of Young People* (Bramcote, Notts.: Grove Books 1985).

Roger Hurding: *Understanding Adolescence* (London: Hodder and Stoughton, 1989).

Bruce Gillingham, *The Christian Student and the Local Church* (Bramcote, Notts.: Grove Books, 1983).

Roger Owen, *Parents Guide 12–16* (Eastbourne: Kingsway, 1988).

Pete Ward, *Youth culture and the gospel* (Basingstoke: Marshall Pickering, 1992).

Bob and Gretchen Pasantino, *When the devil dares your kids* (Guildford: Eagle Books, 1991).

David Day and Philip May, *Teenage beliefs* (Tring: Lion Publishing, 1991).

Peter Brierley, *Reaching and keeping teenagers* (Tunbridge Wells: Monarch MARC, 1993). Based on detailed social survey work on teenagers and religion.

UNEMPLOYMENT

Julian Charley, *Pastoral care for the unemployed* (Bramcote, Notts: Grove Books Ltd, 1984).

Leslie J. Francis, *Young and unemployed* (London: Costello, 1984).

Peter Elsom and David Porter, *4,000,000 reasons to care: How your church can help the unemployed* (Bromley: MARC Europe and Church Action with the Unemployed, 1985).

Michael Moynagh, *Making unemployment work* (Tring: Lion Publishing, 1985).

DEPRESSION

John White, *The Masks of Melancholy* (Leicester: IVP, 1982).

Richard Winter, *The Roots of Sorrow: Reflections on Depression and Hope* (Basingstoke: Marshall, Morgan and Scott, 1985).

Myra Chave-Jones, *Coping with Depression* (Tring: Lion Publishing, 1981).

Martha Maughon, *Why am I Crying?* (Basingstoke: Marshall, Morgan and Scott, 1983).

(It is *essential* that elders who have been fortunate enough not to have experienced prolonged depression should read one or other of these books to gain an insight into the situation of the depressed person.)

ILLNESS AND BEREAVEMENT

Peter Speck, *Being there: Pastoral care in time of illness*, (London: SPCK, 1988).

Alistair McGrath, *Suffering*, (London: Hodder and Stoughton, 1992). Primarily written for ordinands and others involved in pastoral care.

Jean Richardson, *A Death in the Family* (Tring: Lion Publishing, 1979).

Elizabeth Kubler Ross, *On Death and Dying* (London: Tavistock Publications, 1970).

Iaian Ainsworth-Smith and Peter Speck, *Letting go: Caring for the dying and bereaved* (London: SPCK, 1982)

Michael Cole, *Going home*, (Guildford: Highland, 1992).

DIFFERING ABILITIES

Sheila Hollins and Margarety Grimer, *Going somewhere: People with mental handicaps and their pastoral care* (London: SPCK, 1988).

THE OCCULT

Russ Parker, *The Occult . . . Deliverance from Evil* (Leicester: IVP, 1989).

John Allan, *Dealing with Darkness* (Edinburgh: The Handsel Press, 1986).

F. S. Leahy, *Satan cast out: A study in Biblical demonology* (Edinburgh: Banner of Truth, 1975 (reprinted 1990)).

Nigel Wright, *Fair face of evil: Putting the power of darkness in its place* (Edinburgh: Marshall Pickering, 1989).

David Burnett, *Unearthly powers: A Christian perspective on primal and folk religion* (Eastbourne: Monarch MARC, 1988).

David Burnett, *Dawning of pagan moon: An investigation into the rise of Western paganism* (Eastbourne: Monarch MARC, 1991).

CHURCH DISCIPLINE

Marlin Jeschke, *Discipling in the Church: Congregational Discipline according to the Gospel* (Scottdale, Pa: Herald Press, 1988).†

Ronald Kraybill, *Repairing the Breach: Ministering in Community Conflict* (Scottdale, Pa: Herald Press, 1981).

Donald Bridge, *Spare the rod and spoil the church*, (Bromley: MARC Europe, 1985).

John White and Ken Blue, *Healing the Wounded: The costly love of church discipline* (Leicester: IVP, 1985).

CONFLICT RESOLUTION

Harold Rowdon (ed.), *Handling differences*, Christian Brethren Review Journal No. 38 (Exeter: Paternoster Press, 1987).

Pauline Bell and Pauline Jordan, *Handling conflict in the local church* (London: Scripture Union, 1992).

D. TEACHING

J. R. W. Stott, *I believe in Preaching* (London: Hodder and Stoughton, 1982). A comprehensive study for those who want to improve their performance as teachers from the pulpit or on other set-piece occasions.

Denis Lane, *Preach the Word* (Welwyn: The Evangelical Press, 1979, revised edition, 1986). A very helpful, practical book on expository preaching, with assignments for the reader at the end of each chapter.

Peter Cotterell, *Look Who's Talking!* (Eastbourne: Kingsway Publications, 1984). A clear guide to better communications in all kinds of teaching situations in the local church.

Anton Baumohl, *Making Adult Disciples: Learning and Teaching in the Local Church* (London: Scripture Union, 1984). A handbook on the *practice* of Christian teaching across the range of teaching opportunities in the local church.

Brian Butler, *The complete guide to preaching* (Basingstoke: Marshall Pickering, 1989).

Robert Paterson, *Short, sharp and off the point* (Bromley: MARC Europe, 1987).

John Baigent, *Teaching in the Local Church* (Partnership Study Guide No. 1), CBRF Partnership, 1986 (obtainable from the Paternoster Press). A stimulus to group discussion on the nature, purpose, planning and provision of teaching in the local church.

Haddon W. Robinson, *Expository Preaching: Principles and Practice* (Leicester: IVP, 1986).

James Rye, *The Communicator's Craft* (Leicester: IVP, 1990).

Bill Hybels, Stuart Briscoe and Haddon Robinson, *Mastering Contemporary Preaching* (Leicester: IVP, 1991).

Derek Tidball, *On the Bridge: a study guide for preachers and worship leaders* (The Baptist Union of Great Britain, 1992).

E.   LEADERSHIP

Despite the manifest importance of leadership in both the Old and New Testaments, Christian leadership has been a neglected subject until comparatively recently, perhaps because it was assumed in earlier generations that those holding office in the congregation would and should automatically supply this vital ingredient of congregational life. Recently, however, there has been a multiplication of books on the subject, particularly from 'Charismatic' sources, to the point that there is even some danger that it will be done to death by over-enthusiasm, and that congregations will be damaged as a result. For the moment, however, in Brethren congregations the risk is the reverse—of inadequate Christian leadership.

John Perry, *Effective Christian Leadership* (London: Hodder and Stoughton, 2nd edition, 1983).

J. Oswald Sanders, *Spiritual Leadership* (London: Marshall, Morgan and Scott, 1967).

Ted W. Engstrom, *The Making of a Christian Leader* (Grand Rapids: Zondervan, 1976). A book which attempts to draw extensively on U.S. secular literature on managerial leadership to apply it in the Christian context.

David Cormack, *Team Spirit* (Bromley: MARC Europe, 1987). Similar to the previous item, but from a more British perspective.

Philip Greenslade, *Leadership: Patterns for Biblical Leadership Today* (Basing stoke: Marshall, Morgan and Scott, 1984).

Derek Copley, *Taking a Lead* (Eastbourne: Kingsway Publications, 1985).

E. R. Dayton and Ted W. Engstrom, *Strategy for Leadership* (London: Marc Europe, 1985).

Charles Sibthorpe, *A Man under Authority* (Eastbourne: Kingsway Publications, 1984). A challenging book on the qualities required in a Christian leader.

Anton Baumohl, *Grow your own leaders* (London: Scripture Union, 1987).

Eddie Gibbs, *Followed or pushed?* (Bromley: MARC Europe, 1987). Strong encouragement to leaders to lead.

Michael Jacobs, *Holding in Trust* (London: SPCK, 1989). Self appraisal for leaders.

Philip King, *Leadership explosion* (London: Hodder and Stoughton, 1987).

David Cormack, *Peacing Together: From conflict to reconciliation*, (Eastbourne: Monarch MARC, 1989).

John Finney, *Understanding Leadership* (London: Daybreak, 1989). Not to be missed!

Fred Bacon, *Being a Christian Leader*, (London: The Baptist Union of Great Britain, 1990). A useful and practical study guide.

Paul Beesley-Murray, *Dynamic Leadership*, (Eastbourne: Monarch MARC, 1990).

Tom Sine, *Wild Hope: a wake-up call to the challenges and opportunities of the 21st century*, (Tunbridge Wells: Monarch, 1992).

Michael Sluter and David Lee, *The R Factor*, (London: Hodder and Stoughton, 1993).

RECOGNISING AND DEVELOPING GIFTS?

Tom Walker, *Small Streams, Big Rivers* (London: Scripture Union, 1991). Developing spiritual gifts in small groups and the church.

C. Peter Wagner, *Your Spiritual Gifts Can Help Your Church Grow* (Eastbourne: Monarch, 1985).

Michael Griffiths, *Serving Grace* (MARC Europe/OMF, 1986).

Graham Houston, *Prophecy Now* (Leicester: IVP, 1989).

F.   CONGREGATIONAL STRATEGY

This manual has emphasized the importance in elders of vision for the direction in which God wishes them to lead their congregations. Sometimes there is difficulty in grasping what is meant by vision in this respect, and how to make a start in thinking about the directions in which the Lord wishes a particular congregation to develop. The following books may stimulate thought.

David Kornfield, *Church Renewal* (Exeter: The Paternoster Press, 1989). A practical manual covering thirteen aspects of church life.

Eddie Gibbs, *I believe in Church Growth* (London: Hodder and Stoughton, 1981).

Peter Cotterell, *Church alive!* (Leicester: IVP, 1981).

Roy Pointer, *How do Churches grow?* (London: Marshall 1984).

Roy Pointer, *The Growth Book,* (Bromley: MARC Europe, 1987).

C. Peter Wagner, *Leading your Church to Growth* (London: Marc Europe, 1986).

David Holloway, *Ready, Steady, Grow* (Eastbourne: Kingsway, 1989).

George Barna, *Marketing the church: What they never taught you about church growth* (Colorado Springs: Navpress, 1988).

Peter Brierley, *Vision Building* (London: Hodder and Stoughton, 1989).

Fran Beckett, *Called to Action* (London: Collins Fount, 1989). A practical guide to community service as a springboard for evangelism.

Michael Wooderson, *The Church down our Street: A guide to everyday evangelism,* (Eastbourne: MARC, 1989).

Nigel Wright, *Challenge to change: A radical agenda for Baptists,* (Eastbourne: Kingsway, 1991).

John Finney, *The Well Church Book: A practical guide to mission,* (London: CPAS/Scripture Union, 1991).

Kevin Dyer, *Must Brethren churches die?.* (Exeter: The Paternoster Press for Partnership Publications, 1992).

Martin Robinson, *A World Apart: Creating a church for the unchurched,* (Tunbridge Wells: Monarch, 1992). Learning from the Willow Creek experience.

Tom Wright, *New Tasks for a Renewed Church,* (London: Hodder and Stoughton, 1992).

Paul Beesley-Murray, *Radical Believers: the Baptist way of being church*, (Abingdon: The Baptist Union of Great Britain, 1992).

John Finney, *Church on the Move: Leadership for mission*, (London: Daybreak, 1992).

David Cohen and Stephen Gaukroger, *How to close your church in a decade* (London: Scripture Union, 1992). A survey of the rudiments of congregational strategy so as to avoid what many leaders appear to be trying to do!

Peter Brierley, *Priorities, Planning and Paperwork* (Tunbridge Wells: Monarch MARC, 1992). A primer on the mundane practicalities of church leadership.

Harold Rowdon (ed.), *The strengthening, growth and planting of local churches* (Carlisle: Paternoster Press for Partnership, 1993).

Eddie Gibbs, *Winning them back: Tackling the problem of nominal Christianity* (Tunbridge Wells: Monarch MARC, 1993).

Stuart Murray, *The Challenge of the City: A Biblical View*, Tonbridge Sovereign World, 1993).

THE STATISTICAL UNDERPINNINGS OF CONGREGATIONAL STRATEGY

A congregational strategy will be the more effective for being founded on a thorough understanding of those whom we are trying to reach, who they are and the way they are likely to think. Small area census data on a ward or parish basis for April 1991 can usually be obtained from the local library and local authority offices—they contain a wealth of different information about the overall character of each area, with enormous possibilities for cross-tabulation. Survey data and analysis at the national level is given in the following:

Peter Brierley, *'Christian England': What the English Church Census reveals* (London: MARC Europe, 1991).

Michael Fanstone, *The sheep that got away: Why do people leave the church?* (Tunbridge Wells: Monarch MARC, 1993). Turbulence of congregational membership is increasing: this book gives some of the reasons why.

Robin Gill, *The Myth of the Empty Church*, (London: SPCK, 1993). '. . . it is not belief that fosters churchgoing, or disbelief that causes the decline in churchgoing, but churchgoing that fosters belief, and . . . there is nothing inevitable or predestined about the continued decline in church attendance.'

Peter Brierley and Val Hiscock (ed.), *UK Christian Handbook 1994/95 Edition* (London: Christian Research Association, Evangelical Alliance, and the British and Foreign Bible Society, 1993), pp. 237–282.

Peter Brierley, Graham Brown, Boyd Myers, Harold Rowdon and Neil Summerton, *The Christian Brethren as the Nineties began*, (Carlisle Paternoster Press for Partnership in association with MARC Europe 1993). Detailed analyses of recent trends in 'Brethren' congregations.

CHURCH PLANTING

Monica Hill (ed.), *How to plant churches* (London: MARC Europe *et al.*, 1984).

D. W. Shenk and E. R. Stutzman, *Creating communities of the kingdom: New Testament models of church planting*, (Scottsdale, Penn.: Herald, 1993)+. How the churches we plant are to be more than another sort of social club.

Charlie Cleverley, *Church Planting: Our future hope* (London: Scripture Union, 1991).

George Carey *et al.*, (ed. Bob Hopkins and Tim Anderson), *Planting new churches* (Guildford: Eagle Books, 1991).

Martin Robinson and Stuart Christine, *Planting tomorrow's churches today* (Tunbridge Wells: Monarch, 1992).

HOME GROUPS

John Mallinson, *Growing Christians in small groups* (London: Scripture Union, 1989).

Richard Haydon-Knowell, *Leading a house-group* (Milton Keynes: Word (UK) Ltd, 1988).

John Finney, *Groups: Asking the right questions*, Grove Pastoral Series No. 23 (Bramcote: Grove Books Ltd, 1985).

How to lead small group Bible studies (New Malden: Navpress, 1985).

Books which present a challenge as to what the local church ought to be are:–

H. L. Ellison, *The Household Church* (Exeter: The Paternoster Press, 1963, 1979²). A trail-blazing study pointing to a less institutional church community.

Robert Banks, *Paul's Idea of Community: The Early House Churches in their Historical Setting* (Exeter: The Paternoster Press, 1980). A biblical analysis of the New Testament Church with particular reference to community, gifts, and office, which draws extensively on modern biblical studies.

Howard A. Snyder, *New Wineskins* (London: Marshall, Morgan and Scott, 1977). A challenge to examine the man-made structures of the church.

Howard A. Snyder, *The Community of the King* (Downers Grove, Illinois: Inter-Varsity Press, 1977).

Howard A. Snyder, *Liberating the Church* (Downers Grove, Illinois: Inter-Varsity Press, 1983). Argues for a new model of the church aimed at ensuring that it embodies the kingdom of God.

Gerald Coates, *What on Earth is this Kingdom?* (Eastbourne: Kingsway, Publications, 1983). A radical challenge to institutionalization in the church (in the best Brethren tradition!).

Charles J. Mallis, *Committed Communities: Fresh Streams for World Missions* (Pasadena, Cal.: William Carey Library, 1976).

A Noble Task

Jean Vanier, *Community and Growth* (London: Darton, Longman and Todd, 1979).
Robert Roxburgh, *Renewal down to Earth* (Eastbourne: Kingsway, 1987).
Terry Virgo, *Restoration in the Church* (Eastbourne: Kingsway, 1985).
Nigel Wright, *The Radical Kingdom* (Eastbourne: Kingsway, 1986).
Nathan de Lynn Smith, *Roots, Renewal and the Brethren,* (Pasadena: Hope Publishing House and Exeter: The Paternoster Press, 1986).

The following four books are useful in presenting stimulating case studies of the way in which different congregations of different traditions have experienced spiritual blessing:–

Eddie Gibbs (ed.), *Ten growing Churches* (London: Marc Europe & the British Church Growth Association, 1984).
Roger Forster (ed.), *Ten new Churches* (London: Marc Europe and the British Church Growth Association, 1986).
Graham Kendrick (ed.), *Ten worshipping Churches* (London: Marc Europe and the British Church Growth Association, 1986).
Donald English (ed.), *Ten praying Churches* London: Marc Europe and the British Church Growth Association, 1989).

G. WORSHIP

The renewal of worship has been a key aspect of church growth in the present generation, and in my judgment still needs particular attention by leaders of Brethren congregations.

John Baigent (ed.), *Declare His glory: A fresh look at our congregational worship,* Christian Brethren Review No. 39, (Exeter: The Paternoster Press, 1988). Looks specifically at worship in Brethren congregations.
Graham Kendrick, *Worship* (Eastbourne: Kingsway, 1984).
Jock Anderson, *Worship the Lord* (Leicester: IVP, 1980).
John Leach, *Liturgy and Liberty: Combining the best of the old with the best of the new in worship* (Eastbourne: MARC, 1989).
Eleanor Kreider, *Enter His gates: Fitting worship together,* (Basingstoke: Marshall Pickering, 1989).
Phil Rogers, *Learning to Worship* (Milton Keynes: Word (UK) Ltd., 1988).
D. A. Carson (editor), *Worship: Adoration and Action* (Carlisle: Paternoster Press, 1993).
Paul Beasley-Murray, *Faith and Festivity: A Guide for Today's Worship Leaders* (Eastbourne: MARC, 1991).

* Forthcoming, at the time of writing.
† Herald Press books may be obtained from The Metanoia Book Service, 14 Shepherds Hill, London N.6.
‡ Available from Aids to Bible Education, 'Charleville', Harbour Road, Dalkey, C° Dublin, Ireland.

TRAINING OPPORTUNITIES

Chapter 11 noted that it can be difficult for many congregational elders and other leaders to find time for extended periods of full-time study to prepare and develop themselves for more effective discharge of their responsibilities. Where there is a will, there is a way, of course. But for many, formal training and education for eldership will have to be confined to summer schools, weekend courses and day seminars.

Unless I am ill-informed, there are still comparatively few suitable opportunities available. (There is a market gap here into which the colleges ought to move more positively—though a factor is the widespread and regrettable lack of commitment to training on the part of many local church leaders and potential leaders.) The information below is intended to give an indication of some of the opportunities at present available in England. The main purpose is to whet the appetite for training which may expand horizons and challenge elders to more effective service. The list does not pretend to be exhaustive. I hope that the bodies mentioned will benefit through greater take-up of what they have on offer. I take full responsibility for any errors which may have resulted from my efforts to summarise.

* *Partnership* is seeking to give an increasing level of support to independent local churches, particularly those with Brethren origins. It regards the training and development of elders and others in congregational leadership as a primary objective. It organises national consultations from time to time which incorporate training workshops. Recent consultations have given rise to local and regional activities which frequently include training workshops. Partnership is ready to assist in organising local day-seminars, weekend courses and summer schools, whether for individual churches or groups of churches. An

example is the course 'Ready to serve?: an introduction to leadership in the local church' which is being mounted by the North London Partnership Group in the winter of 1994. This is based on a course drawn up by John Baigent (6 Windmill Road, London SW18 2EU (tel.: 081–870 0776)) who has considerable experience in running courses for Brethren churches in SW London and who is available to provide various forms of assistance, including training in church leadership. Partnership also has a panel of consultants who are ready to give advice to local church leaders on request.

(Enquiries on all Partnership activities and services to: Neil Summerton (Executive Secretary), 52 Hornsey Lane, London N6 5LU. Tel.: 071–272 0643.)

* *Counties Evangelistic Work* has established a training department to focus on training in evangelism and is willing to mount courses locally and regionally. In July 1994 it is organising a training weekend, 'Cutting Edge', for people aged between 18 and 30.

(Enquiries to: R. F. Davies, National Administrator, Counties Evangelistic Work, 30 Haynes Road, Westbury, Wiltshire BA13 3HD. Tel.: 0373 823013.)

* *Stepping Stones Christian Training Project* aims to provide supervised training in Christian service for up to 12 months for established Christians in needy but active independent evangelical churches. It is designed to develop leadership qualities and individual gifts in evangelism, teaching, pastoring and counselling. Training is mainly through supervised placements in local churches.

(Enquiries to: John Rogers, 14 Lant Close, Duggins Lane, Tile Hill, Coventry CV4 9TG. Tel.: (0203) 471991.)

* *Workshop* offers a programme of Christian Discipleship and Leadership Training for 'men and women with busy lives; people who have the demands and responsibilities of work, local church and family life'. In 1993/94 the course is running one weekend (Saturday and Sunday) a month in three different locations—Birmingham, Exeter and London. It is non-residential though, if necessary, accommodation can be arranged. This is a type of course which is suited to meeting the training needs of leaders in full-time secular employment, though to my mind it is a pity that, from a reading of the prospectus at least, it does not appear to contain more material on the practicalities of church leadership.

(Enquiries to: David Henthorne, Workshop Enrolment Office,

42 Rossett Green Lane, Harrogate, North Yorkshire HG2 9LQ. Tel.: 0423 871 412.)

* The *Christian Research Association* offers courses from time to time for leaders on, for example, 'Vision Building', 'Priorities, Planning and Paperwork', 'The Sheep that got away', and 'Reaching and Keeping Teenagers'. These build on the CRA's extensive research and survey work. The Executive Director is also willing by arrangement to participate in the planning and delivery of courses arranged by others. Membership of the CRA (£18 per annum) gives access to the CRA's database as well as regular information about its training events.

   (Enquiries to: Peter Brierley, Executive Director, CRA, Vision Building, 4 Footscray Road, London SE9 2TZ. Tel.: 081–294 1989; Fax.: 081–294 0014.)

* *The Oasis/Spurgeon's Church Planting and Evangelism Course* aims to equip men and women for the task of church planting. It is a three-year modular course, requiring attendance one day a week during term time, local church placements and home study. Normally, students combine the course with additional tuition leading to theological qualifications but it is also possible to take the course, or part of it, on its own. From 1994 one and two year courses are also available.

   (Enquiries to: Stuart Murray, Oasis Director of Church Planting and Evangelism, Spurgeon's College, 189 South Norwood Hill, London SE25 6DJ.)

* *Administry* seeks to provide fresh ideas on all aspects of church administration and church leadership through highly-relevant resource papers based on surveys of member churches. Training events, open to non-members, on communications, team working, and how to be a welcoming church are organised in a variety of locations. These can also be booked by individual local churches. Administry is also able to provide consultancy help on the organisation of a local church.

   (Enquiries to: Michael Streeter, National Director, PO Box 57, St Albans, Herts AL1 4AD. Tel.: (0727) 856370.)

* The *Scripture Union Training Unit* offers a 'skeleton' programme of practical training each year on Saturdays in different locations across the country which covers topics such as teamwork, committee work, management of change, managing people, counselling skills, adult learning, small group leadership, as well as family and children's work. The unit also offers courses tailored specifically to meet the needs of individual churches and organisations in all the above topics. 'Talk to us about your

needs . . . fees negotiable', they say. Eleven comprehensive
DIY training packs are also available, on subjects such as
'Christian caring', 'The church and the retired generations',
'Being the church family together', 'Marriage is for life', and
'Leading small groups'.

(Enquiries to: The Training Unit, Scripture Union, 26–30
Heathcoat Street, Nottingham NG1 3AA. Tel.: (0602) 418144.)

Increasingly, the theological and Bible colleges are offering part-
time and extension studies which are practicable for church leaders
whose work and other responsibilities restrict the time available
for training. In my judgment, it will usually be preferable to give
priority to the applied, rather than purely theological, modules.
Training for the Anglican ministry is increasingly being shifted to
a part-time basis, and at least some colleges (e.g., Oak Hill College,
Southgate, London N14 4PS) are willing to accept non-Anglicans
for the courses.

INDEX